Praise for *Hildegard of Bingen*

"Comprehensive.... [A] balanced presentation both of Hildegard's gifts and her weaknesses, revealing her as fully human yet filled up with God."
—**Norvene Vest**, author, *What Is Your Practice? Lifelong Growth in the Spirit*

"An insightful introduction; wisely chosen texts; clear, concise annotation.... Instructs readers how to handle the texts ... on the nun's own terms."
—**Mary Hunt**, coeditor, *New Feminist Christianity: Many Voices, Many Views*

"Writing with clear love of Hildegard von Bingen and from her own perspective as theologian, religious leader and woman of faith, Sheryl Kujawa-Holbrook ... provides a hybrid scholarly and practical resource for anyone seeking to know Hildegard von Bingen and her world."
—**Suzanne R. Ehly**, sporano and former member of *Sequentia*;
artist in residence and faculty in voice, body and culture,
Episcopal Divinity School

"A must-have book for anyone wanting a deep personal experience of Hildegard of Bingen; her life, writings and music; and her faith in God."
—**Rev. Dr. Carole Ann Camp**, coauthor, *Labyrinths from the Outside In:
Walking to Spiritual Insight—A Beginner's Guide*;
founder, Seekers and Sojourners

"The 'best of' Hildegard's writings ... illuminated ... with wise and knowledgeable comments....Anyone of any tradition will enjoy this beautiful book."
—**Sister Greta Ronningen**, cofounder, Community of Divine Love Monastery

"An excellent introduction to [Hildegard's] thought."
—**Rosemary Radford Ruether**, author,
Integrating Ecofeminism, Globulization and World Religions

T0266246

Hildegard of Bingen

Other Books in the SkyLight Illuminations Series

Hildegard of Bingen

Essential Writings and Chants of a Christian Mystic— Annotated & Explained

Translation and annotation by
Dr. Sheryl A. Kujawa-Holbrook

Walking Together, Finding the Way ®
SKYLIGHT PATHS®
PUBLISHING
Nashville, Tennessee

Hildegard of Bingen:
Essential Writings and Chants of a Christian Mystic—Annotated & Explained

2016 Quality Paperback Edition

Translation, annotation, and introductory material © 2016 by Sheryl A. Kujawa-Holbrook

Library of Congress Cataloging-in-Publication Data
Names: Hildegard, Saint, 1098–1179. | Kujawa-Holbrook, Sheryl A., annotator.
Title: Hildegard of Bingen : essential writings and chants of a Christian
    mystic annotated & explained / annotation by Dr. Sheryl A. Kujawa-Holbrook.
Description: Woodstock, VT : SkyLight Paths Publishing, 2016. | Series:
    Skylight illuminations series | Includes bibliographical references.
Identifiers: LCCN 2015039481| ISBN 9781594735141 (pbk.) | ISBN 9781594736223
    (ebook) | ISBN 9781683365471 (hc)
Subjects: LCSH: Mysticism—Catholic Church—Early works to 1800. | Spiritual
    life—Catholic Church—Early works to 1800.
Classification: LCC BX4700.H5 A25 2016 | DDC 248.2/2—dc23 LC record available
    at http://lccn.loc.gov/2015039481

Manufactured in the United States of America

Cover design: Walter C. Bumford, III, Stockton, Massachusetts
Cover art: Hildegard dictating to her scribe, Volmar, as depicted in the frontispiece to the Lucca codex of *Liber divinorum operum* (ca. 1220).

SkyLight Paths Publishing is creating a place where people of different spiritual traditions come together for challenge and inspiration, a place where we can help each other understand the mystery that lies at the heart of our existence.

SkyLight Paths sees both believers and seekers as a community that increasingly transcends traditional boundaries of religion and denomination—people wanting to learn from each other, *walking together, finding the way.*

SkyLight Paths, "Walking Together, Finding the Way" and colophon are trademarks of LongHill Partners, Inc., registered in the U.S. Patent and Trademark Office.

Walking Together, Finding the Way
Published by SkyLight Paths Publishing
An imprint of Turner Publishing Company
4507 Charlotte Avenue, Suite 100
Nashville, TN 37209
Tel: (615) 255-2665
www.skylightpaths.com

To Rachel,
our own "mirror of divinity"

Contents ☐

Contents

Preface ☐

I was on a trip to New York City years ago when I walked into one of my favorite sacred places, the Cathedral of St. John the Divine, and I was instantly mesmerized. The shop in the cathedral was playing the music of Hildegard of Bingen, "A Feather on the Breath of God," performed by Christopher Page, Emma Kirkby, and Gothic Voices. The music was the most spellbinding I had ever heard, and it was soaring throughout that glorious cathedral. It was one of those experiences that the ancient Celts would say "touch heaven." I sat down in a pew and listened to the music of that recording twice through, only leaving in time to purchase a copy. (I also had to buy a CD player on the way home!) As a graduate student in the history of Christianity, I went back to Cambridge and resolved to learn more about Hildegard of Bingen, about her music, and, eventually, about her many works.

This book is the result of my years of Hildegard study since then. Although I have formally studied women medieval mystics, including Hildegard, over the years I have actually used many more of her works than any others in my spiritual direction, preaching, retreat leading, and adult education. Her recent and overdue canonization opened her world to a new generation. Thus, this book is geared to that audience, those who may have been introduced to her through her music, or those interested in spirituality and mysticism. It is my hope that this book will prove useful to others who are beginning to learn about Hildegard, who want an introduction to her copious body of work, or who want to know the background to her memorable music. It is also my hope that, as an introduction to some of her texts, this book will encourage others to do further study and reflection on the life and work of Hildegard of Bingen.

This book would not have been possible without the rich and varied studies and secondary literature available on the life and work of Hildegard of Bingen. My own thirty years of Hildegard study have been enriched by the work of many who have studied and written about this remarkable woman. In particular, I would like to mention the renowned Hildegard scholars Peter Dronke, Bruce Hozeski, Beverly Mayne Kienzle, and Barbara Newman, from whom I have gained incalculable insights, as noted in some of the annotations in this book. An abbreviated list of additional works and a discography appear in the back of this book for further study. This space does not allow me to list all the Hildegard literature available, and I apologize in advance to readers who believe I omitted crucial books, music, or film. If you consult just one website in search of additional works, visit the site of the International Society of Hildegard von Bingen Studies, listed in the Suggested Resources in the back of this book.

This work was supported, in part, through a Conant Sabbatical Grant, provided by the Episcopal Church Center for scholars who teach in Episcopal seminaries. The book would not have been completed without the support of SkyLight Paths, specifically Nancy Fitzgerald and Emily Wichland; when I needed additional time to complete this complex manuscript, Emily graciously gave it to me. Many thanks to the individuals and groups who agreed to read and listen to the texts, and who helped me make some of the selections. It was a great challenge to decide what to include and which texts, though interesting and insightful, to leave out.

As always, I am indebted to my family, Paul and Rachel, who stood by as I spent many nights reading and deciphering Latin texts, a decidedly solitary venture for the most part. They made sure I was fed and watered as needed. They remain my inspiration for what is most holy and most beautiful.

Introduction ☐

We cannot live in a world that is interpreted for us by others.
An interpreted world is not a hope.
Part of the terror is to take back our own listening.
To use our own voice.
To see our own light.

—Hildegard of Bingen

Who Was Hildegard of Bingen?

Hildegard of Bingen was one of the most accomplished women in the history of Christianity, the first German mystic and the precursor of many of the great women mystics of the Middle Ages. She was also a visionary, abbess, writer, composer, dramatist, spiritual adviser, prophet, poet, preacher, and healer. Born in 1098, she was the tenth child (and a "tithe" to the church) of a German noble family in the Rhineland town of Bermersheim, near Alzey, southwest of Mainz. Her parents were Hildebert and Mechtild; her father was a soldier for the Count of Sponheim, and her mother was a noblewoman. Said to be a frail and sickly child, Hildegard was dedicated to the church at birth. Her spiritual gifts were manifest at an early age; for example, "In my third year I saw such a light that my soul trembled, but because I was just an infant, I could say nothing of these things."[1] At the age of five she prophesied the color of a calf in the womb.[2]

Little else is known of Hildegard's childhood before she was taken by her parents to the anchoress Jutta of Sponheim (1092–1126) when she was eight years old. (Interestingly, later in life Hildegard was critical of the practice of child oblation without the child's consent.) Of her nine siblings, others also served the church; her brother Hugo was cantor at the cathedral in Mainz; her brother Roricus was a canon in Tholey; and a sister, Clementa, eventually became a nun in Hildegard's community at Rupertsberg. Near the end of Hildegard's life, we learn that she had a nephew, Wezelin, prior of St. Andrew's in Cologne, who served briefly as one of her scribes from 1173 to 1174.[3]

Mother Jutta, like Hildegard, also came from a prominent family; she was the daughter of the Count of Sponheim and his wife Sophie, who founded a Benedictine abbey near their home in 1101. At the age of twelve, Jutta vowed to God during a grave illness that if she recovered, she would reject all offers of marriage and enter the religious life. Despite her family's objections, Jutta joined a consecrated widow named Uda Gölkheim when she was about fourteen. Jutta was influenced by the monastic reform movement of her era, and chose the stricter asceticism of the anchoritic life over traditional convent life. She was formally professed and enclosed in a cell beside the monastery of Disibodenberg.

Learning the Religious Life

In the Middle Ages, an anchorite was a religious solitary who lived a consecrated life of fasting and prayer, often residing in a single cell attached to a church or a religious house. During Hildegard's era, women anchorites far outnumbered male anchorites. Throughout the region surrounding the monastery of Disibodenberg, a Benedictine men's community, it was not uncommon for women anchorites to be attached to male religious communities; such arrangements supported the mystic, visionary spirituality of the women, in contrast to the more traditional priestly vocations of the monks.

The life of the twelfth-century anchorite was centered on prayer, fasting, and good works. As a child oblate, Hildegard lived in Jutta's cell, where she was shaped by the Benedictine Rule of life through participation in the Divine Office and instruction in Latin, the psalter, the disciplines of prayer, fasting, and penitential rites, as well as the ten-string psaltery and appropriate manual labor. Like the other girls brought by their families to live under Jutta's direction, Hildegard was schooled in "ways of listening, acting, and speaking that have been tried and tested in the refining force of Divine Wisdom."[4]

Monasteries were the most important educational and artistic centers in Hildegard's era, and many new foundations were established in the twelfth century. Young girls in religious communities spent a great deal of time reading and learning; they also would be spinning or sewing, perhaps copying manuscripts, and, of course, praying. As a child growing up adjacent to a Benedictine abbey, Hildegard was immersed in liturgical music from an early age and had the opportunity to sit near the nuns as they sang the Divine Office and the Eucharist for nearly four hours a day. Hildegard's formal education was most likely not up to the standards of the boys her age who intended to be monks, and she considered herself an *indocta*, or unlearned. But her education was certainly superior to the education of girls outside of religious communities. Her works indicate that she not only had knowledge of the Benedictine Rule, but also knew Scripture, especially the prophets, and had access to biblical commentaries, liturgical texts, and the Western church fathers, such as Jerome, Augustine, Gregory, and even Bede, a monk from faraway Northumbria in Britain.

Although Jutta lived the enclosed life of an anchoress, she was in contact with people in the outside world through the window of her enclosure, and through her correspondence, both of which methods would be familiar to Hildegard after living in such close proximity for thirty years. Primarily a mystic and a visionary, Jutta was not a scholar, and Hildegard herself stressed until late in life that her early education was limited, though she was obviously extremely well read, and probably had access to the monastery library. Though self-conscious about her more rustic Latin style, Hildegard believed it important to stress that her visions were genuine, and that she wrote them as she experienced them, not out of academic knowledge.[5]

Growing up in a monastery where both women and men lived together, and therefore were not as cloistered as in a traditional women's community, likely informed Hildegard's education as well. She would have been more familiar with men than other young nuns, which may explain her confidence and assertiveness in dealing with influential men in adulthood. As a girl from a rich family, Hildegard was probably never exposed to the struggles of most ordinary people. As both Jutta and Hildegard were noblewomen, it was likely that a servant was enclosed in the cell with them and any other girls in the community. Although as an adult she would later comment on the lives of laypeople, it was always as an outside observer.

As a child oblate, Hildegard never had the option of marriage. While she never despised the institution of marriage, she believed it an inferior state to virginity, which was to her the truest sign of unconditional devotion to God. In medieval society, girls were under the control of their fathers before marriage, and afterward under the control of their husbands. For women, the religious life was the only acceptable alternative to marriage. Unlike most medieval women who did marry, Hildegard did have advantages; she had the privilege of higher learning, she had greater freedom in her writing, and she had the time to cultivate her spiritual life. She considered virginity a moral virtue, and she appreciated the independence and the status it gave her in the church and in society. After she became an abbess, Hildegard also exercised authority over others and was empowered to direct her community, roles she could not have exercised to the same degree if she had married. As a bride of Christ, Hildegard may have renounced earthly marriage, yet she believed that she and her nuns were among the most privileged in that they were free to follow their vocations to serve God.[6]

At the age of fifteen, Hildegard decided to make her vows and a formal commitment to the Benedictine way of life. Bishop Otto of Bamberg (1060–1139) received her vows, along with Jutta's, on All Saints Day in 1112. Other noble families learned of Jutta and Hildegard's spiritual gifts and began to send their daughters to join them, and the small community of women who lived together beside the monastery of Disibodenberg eventually grew into a double monastery.

When Jutta died in 1136, Hildegard was chosen unanimously, at the age of thirty-eight, to be her successor as *magistra*, or the superior and "teacher" of the nuns. The nuns were governed by Abbot Kuno and the monks of the community. After her death, Jutta was buried in the middle of the chapel floor of the monastery. Soon her tomb became a site of veneration and miraculous occurrences. Just as Jutta's valuable dowry and spiritual fame secured the monastery of Disibodenberg during her lifetime, in death, her tomb became a "celestial portal" for the monks, a doorway between heaven and earth.[7]

Hildegard's World

Hildegard and her religious contemporaries lived during a time of intense change in the European church and European society. The devastation caused by years of repeated plagues, wars, and the consequent famines influenced the way people experienced human life and spirituality. The uncertainties of daily life contributed to the desire for many to cultivate their inner lives and relationship to God. This growth in human consciousness, along with the overall growth in literacy brought by the expanding towns and the new middle class, changed the way people related to the church.

The series of armed conflicts known as the Crusades, fought over a century, began with the preaching of Pope Urban in 1095, imploring Christian leaders to unite in the quest for Jerusalem. By the eleventh century, as conflicts between the papacy and the Holy Roman Emperor escalated, it seemed advisable to many in the church to put ecclesiastical institutions, property, and appointments under the protection of lay rulers to avoid being attacked or besieged as part of the power struggle. At the same time, several movements calling for monastic reform sprang up independently of each other in Germany, France, and Anglo-Saxon England. Individuals and groups pressed to restore the religious life to its original glory, as found in the "life of the apostles"—that is, a life of poverty, community ownership of all property, chastity, and obedience, and, in some cases, itinerant preaching.

Hildegard lived within the traditional model of Benedictine life, with its balanced emphasis on prayer, study, and work that had attracted adherents since the sixth century. The Benedictine way remained influential throughout Hildegard's lifetime; however, the need for reform was apparent to many within the church and beyond. The great amount of wealth held by the largest Benedictine houses, along with their close association with secular rulers and noble families, suggested too much of a preoccupation with worldly agendas. Further, by the time Hildegard was born, many older women's communities were under scrutiny for being "unreformed." Gradually, during the early twelfth century, the system developed whereby women religious were controlled by men, losing the autonomy characteristic of women's communities in earlier eras, when abbesses held the equivalent to episcopal authority in spiritual and practical matters. The major Benedictine reform movements of the Middle Ages—one led by Benedict of Aniane in the ninth century, the Cluniac reform of the tenth century, and the Cistercians of the twelfth century—all sought to exclude women, either because they considered women too weak to live up to the rigors of the Benedictine Rule, or because they believed men were too weak to live in proximity to women.[8]

In the eleventh and twelfth centuries, many holy men and holy women like Jutta of Sponheim turned to the enclosed and contemplative life of the anchorite. But, numerically speaking, the most successful monastic reform movement in Hildegard's lifetime was led by the Cistercians. Known most widely by the reputation of their famous abbot, Bernard of Clairvaux (ca. 1090–1153), the Cistercians sought to return monastic life to its roots, including poverty, solitude, simplicity, and a rigorous adherence to the Benedictine Rule. Concerned with living the apostolic life, or the life of Jesus's closest disciples, the Cistercians were against the church's close association with secular rulers and critical of practices of the secular clergy, such as the purchasing of high offices and clerical marriage. Unlike most movements at that time, the Cistercians allowed lay brothers—that is, men from the lower classes—into the religious life. The number of Cistercian houses expanded rapidly throughout the Continent and England. Overall, the reform movement is said to have increased the number of monasteries tenfold between 1050 and 1150.[9]

In this context, Hildegard became *magistra* of the small community of women attached to the Disibodenberg monastery after Jutta's death in 1136. She did not start with many resources at her disposal, yet she navigated the political and religious crosscurrents brilliantly, even though it took quite a fight to win the nuns their independence. Jo Ann McNamara, a notable scholar of women's monastic history, believes that it was Hildegard's goal to emulate the autonomy and rich liturgical life of earlier women's communities in Germany, such as that of the canoness Hroswitha of Gandersheim (ca. 935–ca. 1002). To achieve this aim, Hildegard "broke from the gender continuum that made women congenitally inferior to men and argued instead for the providential complementarity of weak women and strong men. Like any courtly lady, she sought to disarm predatory men by an appealing show of womanly weakness and need for male guidance."[10]

Hildegard's Visions and Leadership

For Hildegard, midlife was a period of intense productivity. In 1141, her forty-third year, she received a vision from Jesus Christ, instructing her to write and preach about her visions. Initially, this command caused her dread. Hildegard acknowledged that her visions began when she was very young—only three years old—and that she chose, for the most part, not to speak about them. Living at a time of great political and religious upheaval, Hildegard was most concerned that, if she were to share her visions, she would need to have them officially sanctioned by the church. As a woman religious in a patriarchal church and culture, Hildegard risked her own position and even her physical safety, as well as the reputation of her monastic community, if her visions were deemed false or misguided. Up to that point, she had only shared her visions with Jutta and with Volmar, a monk of Disibodenberg, who was her friend, confessor, and first scribe. It was Volmar who later wrote down many of Hildegard's visions as she dictated them. At times, Hildegard also dictated to other nuns in her community.

Volmar was influential in Hildegard's education and expanded her knowledge of Scripture and theology by encouraging her to read sermons and treatises. Most likely, Volmar was the one who taught the community the basics of musical notation. That Hildegard relied on Volmar's help to compose her works does not detract from Hildegard's prodigious accomplishments as an author. At the time, most male monastic authors used secretaries to assist them in composing their works as well.[11] The idiosyncratic and highly personal style of Hildegard's Latin works suggest the fluidity and brilliance of her own authorship.

First encouraged to record her visions by Archbishop Christian of Mainz, Hildegard gained a critical endorsement in 1147 at the Synod of Trier when Pope Eugenius (Eugene) III (r. 1145–1153) examined her visions and authorized her to write and to speak in public as the Holy Spirit moved her. Barbara Newman, one of the world's foremost scholars on the works of Hildegard, notes that not only was she the first woman to receive permission from the pope to write theology, but she was also the only woman of her era to be accepted as an authority on Christian doctrine.[12] Recognition from the pope for her visions, along with Hildegard's growing reputation for prophecy and healing powers, increased her stature throughout the region, attracting more pilgrims and women interested in joining the community at Disibodenberg.

As the number of women who wanted to join Hildegard's religious community grew, so did her desire to move them all to a new place with more independence. It is possible that, given Jutta's strong connection to the monks at Disibodenberg, Hildegard suspected that she would always live in Jutta's shadow and never be free to lead the community according to her own religious vision while remaining at Disibodenberg.

In 1147, Hildegard made the unprecedented move of securing land and founding a new convent intended to be free of the monks' control, despite her ostensible pleas for male guidance. Using the argument of the male reformers, who stressed that men and women religious should be separated, Hildegard agreed, saying the men who were supposed to serve as protectors were instead growing soft, and unable to take their place in complementing women. Jo Ann McNamara argues that "[Hildegard's] theory of gender complementarity enabled her to attribute female vices to men without seeming to usurp masculine prerogatives."[13] To gain her community's autonomy she was willing to downplay her own intellectual gifts and abilities, always insisting that her accomplishments were the result of divine inspiration.

Predictably, Abbot Kuno resisted the move, supported by the Benedictine vow of stability, which stressed that monks and nuns were never to leave the monastery they had entered. He was supported in this position by the monks of Disibodenberg and the prevailing view that women should not be living on their own, much less governing themselves. He also realized that the monastery would lose the lands and dowries provided by the nuns' families should they establish their own community.

When faced with the abbot's refusal to allow the women to leave, Hildegard wrote letters to all her superiors, including the pope, explaining the vision that commanded her to move the community to Rupertsberg. Afterward, she took to her bed for days, stricken with a deep paralysis brought on, she contended, by God's displeasure with the abbot and the monks for interfering with a divine plan. Hildegard's ongoing paralysis, along with her letter-writing campaign to the monastery's superiors, eventually shamed Abbot Kuno, and he let them go, lest he incur more of God's wrath for delaying the move. A few of the noble-born nuns balked at the idea of leaving the comfort of their current home for a more rustic abode, and feared the loss of the monastery's protection. But a majority of the nuns opted to move to the Rupertsberg convent near Bingen in 1150, designating Hildegard as their leader. She won the right to give the nuns a voice in choosing their prioress (the head of their community, directly under the abbot), and refused an advocate to conduct their temporal affairs. Having worn down her opponents, Hildegard secured her foundation through the support of the Archbishop of Mainz, and recognized him as her sole superior in 1152.

Obtaining suitable financing for an independent foundation was one of the hurdles Hildegard needed to confront to establish her community at Rupertsberg. She managed to untangle and transfer the financial arrangements of the nuns' dowries, which their families had given the monastery, and thereby achieved financial independence for her community by 1158, though she had conflicts with Disibodenberg until the end of her life. The support of wealthy patrons, who brought their property to Rupertsberg, secured the project. Her brothers also gave some land to Rupertsberg.[14] Unlike other Benedictine monasteries, "Hildegard did not acquire sovereign rights, slaves, monastic churches or tithes, but cultivated and administered the land alone or with the help of tenants. Her income was supplemented by donations from believers and beneficences for salvation."[15] Eventually, the community not only possessed a beautiful oratory and some stately buildings, but also running water in the workrooms.[16] In 1163 Hildegard secured the protection of Emperor Frederick Barbarossa for her new foundation, and he declared her abbess. Two years later, with a community of fifty nuns, two priests, seven poor women, servants, and guests, a daughter house was founded at Eibingen, near Rüdesheim, across the Rhine from Bingen. Hildegard would visit this house twice a week.[17] The present-day Abbey of St. Hildegard stands on this site.

Hildegard managed to obtain the pope's endorsement for her visions and established an independent foundation in an age when the prevailing agenda was to subjugate powerful women religious and their communities. That Hildegard understood what she was doing became evident in 1175, near the end of her life, when she no longer felt the need to exercise a great deal of caution. Then she told her biographer that she did indeed learn Latin as a girl, though in an unpolished form, and that she understood all that God had revealed to her. "For Hildegard, therefore, 'reform' was a return to the great old days of communities where women served God with song and drama, richly costumed and sleek with good diets and decent comfort," writes McNamara.[18]

Before the thirteenth century the right of abbesses to teach other women was generally accepted practice.[19] Though Hildegard owed much to her mentor and spiritual mother, Jutta, particularly in regard to her contemplative spirituality and social commitments, it is significant that when she became *magistra*, Hildegard favored a balanced and moderate interpretation of the Benedictine Rule over the more rigorous ascetical regimen favored by anchorites. She was more liberal than the monastic reformers of her time, who advocated for a more literal interpretation of the Rule. She rejected poverty for the convent, and favored adjusting customs when appropriate for her community. For example, Hildegard allowed her nuns to wear tiaras, crowns, and white veils on feast days as a celebratory sign of their virginity. Hildegard also believed that the monastic life could become tedious with too long a silence, and hence allowed the nuns to have time to converse with each other.[20] Although Hildegard was criticized by some of her contemporaries for these unorthodox interpretations of monastic practice, she did take her role as spiritual mother and interpreter of the Rule of St. Benedict for her community of nuns very seriously. So seriously, in fact, that some of the nuns complained about her high standards.[21] In addition to the Rule, Hildegard taught Scripture, the church fathers, and the lives of the saints, with a strong emphasis on the importance of the Virgin Mary. During the twelfth century, when Marian devotion became more popular throughout the church, Hildegard went a step further than other writers of the period. Not only was Mary the antithesis of Eve in Hildegard's view, but she was also the source of the highest blessing in all of creation.

Hildegard's body of work is unusually expansive in terms of genre and subject matter for any theologian of the period, woman or man.[22] For Hildegard, God was Love, and she had a direct and intimate relationship with the Divine. Like other twelfth-century theologians, she was interested in cosmology, Trinitarian theology, and church reform. It was considered unusual for women in Hildegard's time to become writers, although it was not unheard of. The great medieval women mystics tended to be recognized more as "vernacular theologians" than as scholastic theologians, professional academics in universities, or even monastic theologians in the Benedictine tradition. Medieval vernacular theologies, produced by those who did not have university educations, were written in native languages for the most part. Many of the most notable vernacular theologians of the Middle Ages were women; for example, the Beguine Hadewijch (ca. 1250) wrote in Dutch, Catherine of Siena (1347–1380) wrote in Italian, and Julian of Norwich (ca. 1341–ca. 1416) wrote in English. Though these great medieval women theologians shared mystical spirituality with Hildegard, Hildegard was distinctive in that her works were written in Latin, and, though clearly informed by her monastic tradition, she also further expanded upon and interpreted her tradition. In this way, Hildegard is more of a monastic theologian than a vernacular theologian. Like other monastic theologians, she was not particularly concerned with the scientific analysis of Christian doctrines, and while she knew Scripture and theology, her visions served as the primary focus in her writing.[23]

Personal Struggles

Part of Hildegard's enduring appeal is that she was not a perfect person. A woman of convention to the extent that she often claimed she was "poor and frail" or a "weak woman," she also relished being in authority and, at times, exhibited the pride, envy, and possessiveness characteristic of other powerful religious and secular leaders. Aware of her high socioeconomic status, she only accepted noblewomen into her community, and was subjected to criticism for elitism. Although she repeatedly apologized for her lack of formal education, she did not have a hard time sharing her opinions, and her writing is intuitive and bold. Her repeated insistence on her lack of formal theological training supported the argument that her visions were both divinely commanded and divinely inspired. While she did not formally study theology—an option not available to women of her time—her works reflect a deep knowledge of Scripture and theology, as well as familiarity with contemporary sources on the arts and sciences. Indeed, there are few religious writers whose works range across as many fields of expertise as Hildegard's do, even today.

In contrast to Hildegard's passionate personality and dynamic leadership were the many illnesses she suffered throughout her life, which were triggered, first, by her early attempts to suppress her visions, and later on by other occasions of stress. Hildegard claimed that her visions left her exhausted and ill, and that she was very susceptible to changes in the weather. She called her visions *pressura*—a term that combines her acknowledgment of physical pain along with the psychological pain of keeping silent about her visions for so long.[24]

From a twenty-first-century vantage point, it is difficult to pinpoint the source of Hildegard's chronic ill health, made all the more ironic because she lived to be over eighty years old. Scholars and physicians suggest that she suffered from severe migraines, which would explain the periods when she was incapacitated and unable to leave her bed. This diagnosis would also explain the experiences of radiant light that accompanied Hildegard's visions, referred to as "visual auras" in medical terms. These auras mimic points of light that shimmer and move, often resembling stars.[25] Like migraine sufferers today, Hildegard suffered from hallucinations, and subsequent periods of blindness and paralysis after an attack. Her crises were cyclical; periods of debilitating illness with deep inner turmoil were followed by periods of relief and euphoria when it became clear to Hildegard what it was she needed to express. Her visions were often couched in symbolic terms, expressed in paintings that pushed viewers toward new ways of seeing. In this sense, her physical maladies created the conditions whereby her visions were awakened. Given the debilitating aftereffects of her condition, it is remarkable that Hildegard did not succumb to her illnesses, but rather was able to utilize her condition as a means to communicate with the Divine, and to find within it a life-giving source of creativity.

By her own admission, Hildegard received her visions while she was mentally "awake, and seeing with the eyes and ears of the inner self."[26] She experienced her visions with her eyes open, without losing consciousness or being out of touch with reality, and the experiences stayed long in her memory. The impact of Hildegard's experiences of the "Living Light" reveal a wide range of feelings and emotions—love, joy, wonder, awe, fear, despair, hope—and, for a time, euphoria—the absence of all pain and sadness. Throughout most of her life, Hildegard was rarely at rest. In this way her visions were both a burden and an experience of the Living Light. Swiss psychologist Carl Gustav Jung recognized in Hildegard an example of a resilient personality, capable of confronting the inner turmoil that accompanies the experience of unity with the Divine without becoming psychotic. He argues that the human unconscious yearns to be drawn into the light, yet at the same time the ego and the persona resist the painful claims consciousness brings with it. As religious studies professor Avis Clendenen notes in an article on Hildegard and Jung: "Many persons pass through such potentially transforming experiences but fail to stay with them long enough to confront the inner turmoil and psychic suffering that accompany the inbreaking of the divine and thus to emerge with greater wholeness of self and direction in life."[27]

In addition to being perhaps the most creative decade in Hildegard's life, the 1150s also began dramatically for her on a personal level. Soon after the move to Rupertsberg, Richardis of Stade (1123–1151), a young nun and one of Hildegard's few close confidantes, was elected abbess of another community in Bassum. Hildegard had enlisted the young nun's assistance while she was working on the *Scivias* (*Liber scivias domini*, Know the Ways of the Lord), the first of three works describing her visions, as both a collaborator and a support system, until the book was completed.[28] There are various interpretations about the conflicts around Richardis's acceptance of the new position. Some scholars suggest that

Richardis felt pressured into taking the position and was unable to stay at Rupertsberg against her family's wishes. Another interpretation is that Richardis was ready for more freedom and status, and although she had great love and respect for Hildegard, she believed that she would never come into her own under the older nun's control. Heartbroken and desperate at the thought of losing Richardis, Hildegard was adamant that the young nun's departure was *not* the will of God and set about demanding her return. In Hildegard's *Vita*, she accounts for Richardis's decision to leave Rupertsberg as follows: "[B]ecause of her high-born station she felt inclined toward a dignity of greater repute, so she was named the mother of a certain celebrated church which, however, she sought not according to God, but according to the honor of this world."[29] Appeals to Richardis's brother Hartwig, the archbishop who arranged his sister's election as abbess in his own diocese, and the Archbishop of Mainz were rejected. Both men told Hildegard that she needed to let the young woman go. Eventually, Richardis did plan to return to Rupertsberg to be reunited with Hildegard and her community, but the young nun became ill, and tragically died in October 1152 before a reconciliation could be effected.

The temper and possessiveness Hildegard displayed when faced with Richardis's departure has prompted scholars to question the nature of the relationship between the two women. Richardis came into Hildegard's care when she was sixteen, and by all accounts was an extremely gifted pupil. Clearly the two women formed a deep bond. Was theirs a mother-daughter relationship? Did Hildegard consider herself Richardis's spiritual mother in the same way Jutta was a mother figure to Hildegard? In Hildegard's *Vita* the relationship is compared to the relationship between Paul and Timothy in the New Testament.[30] Was it a special friendship between two women religious with similar callings or was it a lesbian relationship?

Scholars have noted that the pattern of homoerotic language by medieval women that derives from the Song of Songs is also found in Hildegard's letters to Richardis, suggesting that the relationship may have been a homoerotic attachment. That Hildegard uses the language of erotic desire to express her devotion to the Virgin Mary further suggests that she did not understand eroticism in the same way as it is understood today, and that it is difficult for us to fully grasp her meaning without relying on modern interpretations.[31]

Two major influences on Hildegard and other devotional writers of the twelfth century were the biblical Song of Songs and Bernard of Clairvaux's sermons on that text. While all devotional writers of the era were influenced by these two sources, the women writers who experienced mystical encounters and recorded them appeared to have been influenced the most. Although Hildegard and Bernard of Clairvaux probably never met in person, they were in correspondence with each other, and she had read his sermons because she quoted them in her letters. Frequent use of bridal mysticism, as well as echoes of the eroticism found in the Song of Songs, are evident in Hildegard's writings. Although Bernard avoids sexualizing the relationship between the soul and Christ in his own writing, he may have prompted the sensual imagery and the erotic language in Hildegard's works, and through her other medieval mystical writers of the twelfth century, such as Elisabeth of Schönau (1129–1164) and Mechtild of Magdeburg (ca. 1207–ca. 1294), both of whom refer directly to Hildegard.[32] During Hildegard's time, women's mysticism was a new concept, and much that was subsequently written on the subject was prompted by her works.

There is no way of knowing exactly how Hildegard and Richardis characterized their relationship. Documents reveal Hildegard as a person who did not have many intimate friends, other than Jutta, Volmar, and Richardis. The whole episode reveals another side of Hildegard's personality, namely, her vulnerability and loneliness. Perhaps because of her brilliance, distinctiveness, and creativity, she was not the kind of person who cultivated many deep friendships. Most of the people she encountered as an adult were in some way subordinate to her as members of her religious community or servants, or they were people from outside her community coming to her for advice. In addition to facing physical health

out her life, Hildegard may have struggled with loneli-

~~ice~~

~~l~~egard attributed the painful drama as a temptation
~~to enjoy~~ ~~l~~res of the world, and her spiritual need to be brought
closer to God. Though sad and distressed, Hildegard survived the episode by focusing on her work. "[T]hose who love me wondered why
God gave me no consolation for I did not wish to persevere in sins, but
by God's help to do good deeds. In these circumstances I completed the
book *Scivias*, as God wished," says the *Vita*.[33]

Hildegard's Influence on the World Outside the Abbey

Hildegard lived during a period of rapid expansion in the monastic life.
As abbess, her reputation became known in ever-widening circles. In this
time of intense civic and ecclesiastical turmoil, she corresponded with
numerous prelates, four popes, emperors, heads of state, and other spiritual figures. Though considered a prophet by some of her contemporaries, Hildegard nevertheless worked from within church structures to
address the worst ecclesiastical abuses of her day, including the increasing
corruption of the church. "In the eleven hundredth year after the Incarnation of Christ, the teaching and fiery justice of the Apostles, which
Christ has established among the Christians and spiritual people, began to
slow down and turn into hesitation. I was born in those times."[34] Church
leaders disagreed about a variety of issues, including the centralization of
papal power, clerical celibacy, and canon law. During these years of religious ferment, Hildegard was actively sought out for her spiritual counsel,
practical advice, and passionate zeal for reform. A notable historian of
women, Gerda Lerner, writes: "The life of Hildegard of Bingen exem-
plifies the breakthrough of a female genius who managed to create an
entirely new role for herself and other women without ostensibly violat-
ing the patriarchal confines within which she functioned."[35]

Unlike other medieval monastics, Hildegard was not completely cloistered and undertook four journeys to monasteries and cathedrals, known

as "preaching tours," between 1159 and 1170, to give spiritual a‹ and to teach women and men. As was often the case, her illnesses werᵂ connected to her prophetic voice, and during these same years she was challenged by intense recurring illnesses; one particularly long spell lasted from 1158 to 1161.

For a woman of her era to teach in public was extraordinary, and it is a testament to Hildegard's spiritual authority and the high regard in which she was held. By the end of the twelfth century, the question of who had the right to preach grew in intensity, in part because heretical groups such as the Waldensians, a Christian movement centered on voluntary poverty and lay preaching, were known for allowing women to preach in public.[36] Though Hildegard did not engage in public speaking on the same scale as male religious, she was the only medieval woman authorized by the church to preach before audiences of both clergy and laity.[37] During her travels she visited many of the cities in Germany, proclaiming the need for church reform and the consequences for those who did not heed God's warnings. Hildegard attributed her ability to preach to the gift of prophecy.[38] The journeys also speak to Hildegard's indomitable will. To travel great distances despite her advanced age and the difficult travel conditions would not even be considered by others with less drive or commitment.

Hildegard began preaching by addressing monastic communities, probably in their chapter houses, in locales along the River Main such as Siebert and Zwiefalten. She demanded that monastic communities live in accordance with the highest standards of their vocation, and was known to offer harsh criticism when she felt it was warranted. Overall, her preaching left a profound impression on her audiences, and many asked for copies of her sermons. She also spoke in Trier, Metz, and Krauftal. At the age of sixty-five she embarked on her most ambitious speaking tour, traveling through Cologne, Boppard, Andernach, Siegburg, Werden, and Liège. During her last tour in 1170, Hildegard covered nearly two hundred miles as she traveled to Swabia, visiting many monasteries along the way.

Griefs in Later Life

After Richardis's departure, Hildegard was again plunged into grief upon the death of her oldest friend and scribe, Volmar, in 1173. The good monk had served her for almost sixty years. After much searching, she found a replacement secretary, the monk Gottfried of Disibodenberg, in late 1174 or early 1175. Gottfried also began working on a biography of Hildegard, but this work was cut short with his death in 1176. Shortly before this, Hildegard had begun a correspondence with the monk Guibert of Gembloux, in present-day Belgium. Guibert became Hildegard's secretary in 1177 and remained in that position until shortly after her death.

When Hildegard was eighty and in the last year of her life, her community was placed under an interdict for allowing the burial of a man suspected of excommunication in their cemetery. Following local custom, the convent at Rupertsberg allowed the burial of local nobility in their cemetery. The religious authorities in Mainz demanded that the man's body be removed from sacred ground. Hildegard, on the other hand, believed that the man had been reconciled with the church before his death, and thus it would be a sin to disturb his grave. Hildegard's response to the order to exhume the body was to take her abbatial staff and wipe out all traces of the grave so it could not be found.[39] The nuns were denied the Mass and the right to sing the Divine Office, except in undertones behind closed doors. Hildegard and her community were literally silenced. The loss of the sacrament and of music was a bitter deprivation for Hildegard and her community, and she confronted church officials with the gravity of their actions. To be deprived of the Mass and music was exile from the symphony of creation. Yet she also thoroughly believed that, despite the interdict, her community's ability to praise God could not be silenced by a command to halt external expression. Rather, Hildegard reasoned, there were many ways to praise God. Singing, dancing, and playing musical instruments are some of these ways, but they could also praise God by speaking in a low voice as they were forced to do. Characteristically, Hildegard sent off letters to her friends in the church hierarchy, and the interdict was eventually lifted in March 1179 by Archbishop Christian of Mainz.[40]

During her last years there were periods when Hildegard was so ill that she was unable to stand and had to be carried from place to place, but her mind remained active and she continued to teach and to write. When Hildegard died six months after the interdict was lifted, on Sunday, September 17, 1179, her sisters testified that at dusk a bright light appeared in the sky, streaming into the room where she lay. The bright light was formed by two brilliant rainbows, which widened to the size of a huge pathway and extended to all four corners of the globe. Where the two rainbows met, the bright light took the form of a circular moon that dispelled all darkness over the Rupertsberg community.[41] Hildegard was buried in the monastic church, and lay there until 1632, when, during the Thirty Years' War, the Rupertsberg convent was destroyed by the Swedes and her relics were moved to Eibingen. Today her heart and tongue are preserved in a golden reliquary in the parish church of Eibingerstrasse in Rüdesheim on the Rhine.

Recognition after Death

Two versions of Hildegard's biography were written around the time of her death, as evidence to future generations of her sanctity. One version was written during the latter years of her life by Guibert of Gembloux, Hildegard's secretary after Volmar's death and an avid supporter, who completed what would come to be known as book one in the fuller biography that was eventually compiled. The second version was begun prior to her death by Gottfried, the provost of Disibodenberg, and Theodoric of Echternach Abbey, who completed books two and three in the decade after Hildegard's death.

While Hildegard was called the "Sybil of the Rhine" and the "Jewel of Bingen" by some of her contemporaries, she was also a controversial figure to some; this sense of controversy grew after her death. Although considered a saint by many after her death, her sainthood was not formally recognized by the Roman Catholic Church until 2012. A protocol was written in support of her canonization in 1223, but neither Gregory IX (1227–1241) nor Innocent IV (1243–1254) gave their approval. The idea of canonizing her was quickly forgotten and her accomplishments systematically minimized. Some even claimed that her work was not her own, or that her visions were the result of a "hysterical" woman. Although her cult was sanctioned by the Avignon papacy, and her name appears in a sixteenth-century book of saints, Hildegard was mostly forgotten until 1940, when her feast day was approved in German dioceses.

The late twentieth-century revival of interest in Hildegard resulted in further investigations that led to her canonization. Although Pope John Paul II canonized more saints than all previous popes combined, he chose to overlook Hildegard. Interestingly, Pope Benedict XVI, who instituted a more arduous canonization process for sainthood and who censured feminist nuns, proclaimed Hildegard of Bingen the thirty-fifth Doctor of the Church on Pentecost Sunday, May 10, 2012. This was an honor previously extended to only three other women saints in Christian history— Catherine of Siena (1347–1380), Teresa of Avila (1515–1582), and Teresa of Lisieux (1873–1879).

Hildegard's Writings

Hildegard was a prolific writer and produced works in a wide variety of genres throughout her life. She is the first saint whose official biography includes her own first-person memoir.[42] Her first public work, *Scivias* (Know the Ways of the Lord), was compiled over the course of a decade, between the years 1141 and 1151, and documents her visions and her interpretations of them. The first of her three visionary works, *Scivias* records twenty-six visions, covering a wide range of topics, including the nature of the universe; the nature of humanity and the human life cycle; the nature of the soul; and the relationship among God, creation, humanity, and the church and the sacraments. The work begins with a declaration: "These are true visions flowing from God." The rest of the *Scivias* is divided into three sections: "The Creator and Creation"; "The Redeemer and Redemption"; and "The History of Salvation Symbolized by a Building." Some Hildegard scholars refer to the *Scivias* as her masterwork because it is a comprehensive analysis of her views on the interrelationships between God, the world, and humanity.[43]

The *Scivias* manuscript is illustrated with illuminations, some resembling mandalas, which accompany each vision. (The original manuscript was destroyed in World War II, though a facsimile, made between 1927 and 1933, is extant.) It is likely that the illuminations were done by a member of Hildegard's community, whom she instructed on what to draw, rather than by Hildegard herself.

Hildegard's style throughout the *Scivias* is passionate and symbolic; she encourages the reader to enter her world through images and metaphors. Her intention is pastoral rather than academic. Deeply concerned about the amount of corruption in church ranks, Hildegard based her agenda on the desire to transform the life of the church as the embodiment of God's work on earth. Hildegard tends to be an optimist. Although she is critical of the church, she could never envision a world without the church in it; thus, she does not overlook its great beauty even in the midst of great challenges.

Hildegard's second visionary work, *Liber vitae meritorum* (Book of the Rewards of Life), written between 1158 and 1163, is a treatise on vices and virtues. It focuses on the nature of sin, the correlation between sins and virtues, and the ways in which sin separates humankind from God. Throughout the work, she presents thirty-five antithetical pairs of sins set against virtues, such as strife and peace, impiety and piety, unhappiness and blessedness. God is the one who gives the universe power and light; all of creation, of which humanity is the highest form, receives life from the Trinity. If we accept the invitation to distance ourselves from evil and live a virtuous existence, we may enter a life of joy. Some scholars consider this to be Hildegard's masterpiece rather than *Scivias*.

Her third visionary work, *Liber divinorum operum* (Book of the Divine Works), written between 1163 and 1173, is her most ambitious. It is based on the few times she experienced an ecstatic loss of consciousness while having her visions. Completed around the time of her dear friend Volmar's death, and therefore very difficult for Hildegard to finish, the work recounts ten cosmological visions. Inspired by the prologue of the Gospel of John, it focuses on the theme of the unity of all creation and the centrality of humankind in God's plan for salvation. In it, the voice of heaven commands Hildegard to transmit, for the good of humanity, all she sees with her inner eye and all she hears with the inner ear of her soul.

In addition to her visionary works, Hildegard wrote two scientific and medical works during the years 1151 to 1158; these were combined into the *Liber subtilitatum diversarum naturum creaturam* (Book on the Subtleties of Many Kinds of Creatures). The two works are *Cause et cure* (Cause and Cure; also known as *Liber compositae medicinae,* Book of Compound Medicine) and *Physica* (Physical Things; also known as *Liber simplices medicinae*, Book of Simple Medicine). Hildegard also had a wide reputation as a healer, attracting to her monastery large numbers of pilgrims and suffering people, who came seeking medical care. These works were in regular use until the fifteenth century,[44] and Hildegard's remedies are still practiced today in the Hildegard Practice, a clinic in Konstanz, Germany.

Unlike her spiritual works, in which she focuses on the supernatural, in her scientific works Hildegard examines observable conditions, and the amount of empirical detail indicates a degree of scientific observation rare for the period. Neither contains references to her visions. Hildegard benefited from having been raised in the Benedictine tradition, which has a long history of tending the sick and cultivating medicinal herbs. Her scientific works suggest that she had a familiarity with the way medicine was practiced in monastic houses. Her sources are unknown; scholars suggest she may have had access to Latin and vernacular texts, though there is no evidence she knew about Arabic medical sources. That a nun was writing about medicine at all was quite remarkable; there is only one other documented female medical writer from the twelfth century, Trotula (d. ca. 1097) of Salerno, Italy.

The first text, *Cause et cure*, is a handbook on the diagnosis and treatment of various diseases, with chapters on human physiology, sexuality, and what is now known as psychology. The second text, *Physica*, is a handbook of healing agents; here she describes the qualities of specific plants, animals, elements, metals, fish, birds, trees, and the like. Throughout both texts, Hildegard expands on current medical knowledge, and she seeks to position healing within the context of both religion and science. Overall, the tone of these works is practical; Hildegard believed that medical knowledge was vital because it relieved suffering, and that practicing healing was an important demonstration of the church's work in the world.[45] Her medicine is based in observation, and the effect of the four seasons on plants, animals, and human bodies. Hildegard stresses throughout her exposition on natural history her belief that humankind is the peak of God's creation. In her view, disease is a symptom of humankind's fall from grace. Her scientific views are based on humoral medicine and the ancient Greek cosmology of the four elements—fire, air, water, and earth—with their four qualities of heat, dryness, moisture, and cold. The body was also thought to be made of four humors: choler (yellow bile), blood, phlegm, and melancholia (black bile). Illness upsets the balance of humors in the body, and the goal of medicine is to restore balance to the body. The system is a holistic one, deeply rooted in horticulture, which corresponds with the rural world in which Hildegard lived.[46]

A distinctive feature of Hildegard's writings on the human body is her generally positive view of sexuality and procreation for her time. Written from a woman's perspective, these texts include one of the first descriptions of the female orgasm. However, she also believed that the life of a consecrated virgin was superior to married life. Though human sexuality is a metaphor for divine love, she believed that nuns were like the Virgin Mary, and therefore fruitful without intercourse.[47]

Hildegard wrote a range of shorter theological, hagiographical, and devotional works geared for religious communities. *Explanatio symboli Sancti Athanasii* (Explanation of the Symbol of Saint Athanasius, ca. 1170) and *Explanatio regulae Sancti Benedicti* (Explanation of the Rule of Saint Benedict, ca. 1150s–early 1160s) were written for the Benedictine monastery of Huy in Belgium. Hildegard's hagiographical works included *Vita Sancti Ruperti* (The Life of Saint Rupert, 1170–1173) and *Vita Sancti Disibodi* (The Life of Saint Disibod, 1170), written near the time of Hildegard's fourth and final preaching tour in Swabia. Hildegard's writings from the 1170s, the last decade of her life, tend to be shorter works than those she wrote in previous decades, yet they bespeak her mature confidence in her visions and in her religious authority.

After 1170 much of Hildegard's written work was in the form of letters or homilies. Among Hildegard's less famous writings are her exegetical works, *Expositiones Evangeliorum* (Homilies on the Gospels), written in the 1160s and '70s, while she was teaching groups of men and women in monasteries and cathedrals. These include fifty-eight allegorical homilies on twenty-seven scriptural passages and liturgical occasions. Perhaps her least-studied work is *Solutions triginta octo quaestionum* (Solutions to Thirty-Eight Questions), a scriptural and theological commentary that resulted from her friendship with the monk Guibert of Gembloux two years before her death. Guibert took it upon himself to repeatedly press Hildegard for answers to difficult questions related to Scripture, and to enlist other monks in the cause: World-renowned Hildegard scholar Beverly Mayne Kienzle argues that Hildegard had three visions that included a mandate from God to Hildegard to share her insights on Scripture, in 1141, 1163, and 1167.[48] "We know of no other twelfth-century woman, and perhaps no other medieval woman, who wrote in standard genres of exegesis—homilies and *solutions*—and whose interpretations of Scripture were sought by male audiences," writes Kienzle.[49] Though it was common for women in monastic communities to request exegetical letters from male teachers, Hildegard is the only women known among her contemporaries to author such letters for men's communities.[50]

Hildegard wrote nearly four hundred letters to popes, bishops, kings, monks and nuns, abbots, and abbesses, as well as women and men from various levels of society throughout Germany and abroad, including luminaries as diverse as Eleanor of Aquitaine (1122–1204); Henry II of England (r. 1154–1189); Abbot Suger (1081–1151); and Frederick Barbarossa, Holy Roman Emperor (r. 1152–1190). Hildegard's letters demonstrate that she had a reputation for wisdom and intelligence beyond her religious community, and they contain spiritual teachings, political commentaries, short sermons, and prophecies, and often direct advice, exhortations, or expressions of moral indignation.

Hildegard witnessed the frequent abuses of church and state in her era, and though she would often describe herself as a "poor woman" she did not shrink from giving a frank appraisal of situations as she saw them. She was frequently appalled by the moral laxity she saw in Christian rulers in both church and state and was concerned with the degree of neglect shown to God's people, and indeed, the abuse of the whole of creation. On more than one occasion, she exhorted a correspondent to "Wake up!" Here Hildegard is speaking about the necessary conditions for a spiritual awakening, or heightened level of consciousness, when our brain activity is heightened, our perceptions are more acute, and our mental functions, like thought and imagination, are the most engaged. An awakening entails moving from a lower to a higher degree of attention in shaping our lives. Hildegard knew that a spiritual breakthrough often comes only after years of questioning and struggle.

On a superficial level, many of Hildegard's terms may seem out of touch with twenty-first-century sensibilities. Terms found in traditional Christian spirituality, like *obedience, humility,* and *surrender,* seem old-fashioned, or even destructive. But she is not talking about the loss of autonomy in human relationships, or the need for arbitrary submission to human power structures. Like other mystics throughout history, Hildegard is describing the need to surrender control in order to completely open our hearts and minds to God.[51] Further, Hildegard does not reserve her advice strictly for the rich and the powerful. She believes that a disciplined spiritual life is necessary for all who seek true happiness; she also believes that all people need to resolve their interior frustrations before well-being can be attained.[52]

Hildegard's Music

Hildegard of Bingen was the first composer of her era known by name, and music she composed was an integral expression of her spirituality. Her experience of God was inextricably linked to music. Hildegard believed that music was not only a form of prayer but also a reflection of the songs of the angels in celestial harmony, and one of the means by which humanity could capture a glimpse of the joy of paradise. Like her visions, Hildegard claimed that most of her music came to her directly from God. Hildegard wrote songs for a variety of liturgical celebrations that were sung by her community and known beyond the monastery. Her music, which dovetailed with her theological writing, was written specifically in response to the needs of a women's religious community and sung daily in their chapel.

Hildegard was also the first composer in Western Europe known to have supervised the copying of her complete musical works. Unlike other chants in her era, Hildegard's chants were carefully copied in heightened notation, which can be read today. She realized that the complexities of her compositions would be difficult to reconstruct through memory alone. Two manuscripts of Hildegard's chants survive—one for use in her community and another reproduced for a men's community in present-day Belgium.[53]

The collecting of Hildegard's musical settings and her poetry had begun by the early 1150s. The settings themselves may date from a period as early as the 1140s; we know that her compositions were known beyond Rupertsberg by 1148. Until the past thirty years, Hildegard's music was largely ignored by musicologists because her unique style made it hard to reconcile with the work of other medieval composers. The poetry of her texts is infused with the images found in her visions, vibrant with light and color, and her music is constructed of varying formulas over an extremely wide vocal range (up to two octaves), with large leaps and complicated melodies, especially well suited to the nuns.[54]

Hildegard's musical compositions include two large works: the *Ordo Virtutum* (Play of the Virtues) and *Symphonia armonie celestium revelationum* (Symphony of the Harmony of Celestial Revelations), also known as the *Symphonia*. The *Ordo Virtutum*, together with Hildegard's *Symphonia*, were collected into a song cycle sometime in the late 1150s.

The *Ordo Virtutum* is the earliest known morality play, a creative art form found in women's monastic communities. With eighty-two melodies, it was composed around the time that Hildegard's dear Richardis moved to Bassum to be the abbess there. *Ordo Virtutum* tells of the struggles of a pure soul, Anima, as she wrestles with worldly temptations brought on by the Devil, Diabolus. The soul must be brought back to God through the intervention of almost twenty virtues, depicted as allegorical figures that help the penitent resist temptation. The virtues are found in biblical literature, as well as in the Benedictine Rule—charity, humility, obedience, chastity, hope, and the like. The play was likely performed by Hildegard and her nuns for the consecration of the monastery church at Rupertsberg in 1152, given that there were as many solo parts for women as there were nuns in the community. The one male solo part in the play is that of the Devil, likely played by the only man at Rupertsberg, Volmar, Hildegard's scribe. That the play was intended for an elaborate occasion is confirmed by her *Scivias*, where Hildegard specifies the colorful costumes and jewelry intended for each character.[55]

Although she sang and composed chants, Hildegard claimed that she never formally studied music. However, the Divine Office sung throughout the day and night were central to the Benedictine life of Hildegard

and her sisters and required some musical training for all the nuns, probably in the novitiate. Hildegard composed most of her music for the Divine
Office; hence, her compositions were shaped by the liturgy. The largest
group of works included antiphons, short pieces of text sung before and
after a psalm, and responsories, texts with music sung after a Scripture
lesson, either by a soloist or by a group. Hildegard also wrote sequences,
or pieces sung between the Alleluia and the Gospel, and hymns, devotional pieces composed with or without melodic repetition.[56]

While Hildegard and her nuns may have lacked formal musical training, they nonetheless lived in an environment that supported women in
the liturgical arts far beyond the level of access afforded to women outside the convent. Thus, Hildegard found a natural outlet for her musical
creativity and her love of music within the confines of the daily religious
life of her community. At least some of her music was also used in the
liturgy at Rupertsberg, at Disibodenberg, in Trier, and at the Cistercian
monastery of Villers that received a manuscript as a gift in 1175.[57]

Hildegard's songs were yet another expression of her profound
sense of unity with the Divine. Of Hildegard's seventy-seven *Symphonia*,
seven are sequences. Most of Hildegard's sequences are borrowed from
a paired-line structure. For sequence texts, she borrowed from Scripture,
her own theology, or the lives of local saints. Hildegard also wrote five
hymns, which, characteristically of her personality, do not fit the traditional pattern. Hildegard's hymns are divided into stanzas, like traditional
hymns, but none has a regular number of lines in a stanza or syllables per
line. Hildegard's hymns also involve different music for each stanza. She
composed forty-three different antiphons and responsories, which com-
prised her largest body of music. In addition to the sequences, hymns,
antiphons, and responsories, Hildegard wrote some songs, either for use
in the Mass or as stand-alone songs devoted to her nuns for the purposes
of praise and contemplation, rather than for use in the liturgy.[58]

Hildegard celebrated the saints in her music. She especially venerated
the Virgin Mary and local saints, such as St. Disibod and St. Rupert. She also

composed a group of songs dedicated to St. Ursula and her companions. The texts and the music of Hildegard's songs are said to be inseparable, focusing the listener on the deeper meaning behind both words and music. As such, the songs are designed as a form of contemplative practice.[59]

In the 1150s, Hildegard also created the *Lingua ignota*, a unique, private language combining German and Latin words that appears in her songs. The language had a twenty-three-letter alphabet and was composed of some nine hundred to a thousand words that she shared only with her nuns. Considered by some to be one of the earliest known constructed languages, the exact use of or audience for the language is unknown. Hildegard may have intended it to be a utopian or universal language of sorts. Another hypothesis suggests that the special language, along with their use of special clothing, was a way of distinguishing the nuns at Rupertsberg from those at other convents and enhancing their sense of having a special vocation. Hildegard scholar Anne H. King-Lenzmeier argues that the language had a liturgical purpose and that its use enhanced ritual celebrations. It served as a means of bonding together the nuns who understood it in terms of their special vocations: "It is Hildegard's vision of the intimate connection between the life of the dedicated virgin, the celestial link through music, and the monastic life as a constant place for practicing the presence of God, the Living Light, which eventually after death would come to be known in full."[60]

Suggestions for Reading Hildegard's Texts

One caveat before reading Hildegard's texts: She is not an "easy" read; that is, her writings are not naturally accessible to a twenty-first-century audience. Hildegard was truly remarkable, and yet, like us all, she was a person of her time and place. Her texts should be approached with a sense of openness and with a willingness to enter her world, to hear her voice in the text. Only then are her words translatable into our era. Oftentimes, the quotations most circulated from Hildegard are rightly acknowledged for their passion and timeless message. But they are taken out of context of the works themselves. Less well known are the writings that reflect her religious orthodoxy, her literal belief in the Devil, or her social elitism, for example. What was truly remarkable about her, however, was her ability to address the many challenges and tribulations of her own time, across an incredible breadth of disciplines, and to such a wide audience. She was a woman with religious authority in a day and time when few gained such stature, and in order to exercise her gifts in such a public capacity, she had to walk a narrow path.

The translations I offer here are close to her original writings, but they are not word for word. Instead, an effort has been made to capture the essence of her message and her spirit in her own worldview. While not a literal translation, language is deliberately chosen to reflect the spirit and intention of the author. The titles are not Hildegard's, but my own, to help the reader better frame the text. When possible, I have made some of the language more inclusive—in particular, when Hildegard discusses *man* but means *humanity* or *humankind*—if it does not change the meaning of the overall text.

Many of Hildegard's writings are passionate, poetic, and mystical; thus, it should not surprise the reader that she uses a great deal of allegorical and symbolic language. Hildegard's works are multidimensional and filled with vivid color and light; her music soars high and plunges into the depths. She lived in religious communities from the time she was a little girl, and there she nurtured and expressed her mystical, creative, and intellectual gifts within a deeply Christian framework. Her texts are evocative and intended to be read and savored reflectively.

Each text is accompanied by annotations to give the reader insights into the context and background of the text and Hildegard's cosmology and theology. Hildegard's writings are filled with biblical allusions and quotations, and pointing them all out would be an endless task, but I do offer relevant Scripture passages that I believe will be of particular interest or that will help explain Hildegard's meaning. All biblical quotations are given in the King James Version, which is the closest and most accessible

English equivalent to the Vulgate, the Latin version of the Bible that Hildegard would have used.

Now, over nine hundred years after Hildegard's birth, there is renewed interest in her writings and her music. The timing is good for a book that introduces the astute spiritual reader to Hildegard's life and a broad range of her major works, grounded in the available scholarship and accessible to readers within the church, as well as those who are not formally religious but have an interest in mysticism, the spiritual life, and feminist and eco-spiritualities, or who are drawn to Hildegard through the arts, particularly her music. The purpose of this book, then, is to introduce a selection of Hildegard's works, annotated and explained, and grouped by theme.

This focus has several advantages. First, in this introductory volume, the reader finds a wider range of Hildegard's works than is typically provided. Also, because the themes of Hildegard's works evolve across genres, the book offers a deeper look at a specific theme than one genre alone can represent. Texts are grouped topically, according to primary themes that run throughout her works.

Finally, this book gives the reader some suggestions about how to read or "listen" to medieval mystical texts. There are some excellent scholarly works examining Hildegard's life and some fine translations of her texts. Yet, in my experience, those new to medieval mystical texts need to learn *how* to read them to understand them on a deeper level. In their enthusiasm for Hildegard, some authors interpret her life in twenty-first-century terms, viewing her as a modern feminist or a rock star. While these characterizations are intended to be complimentary, the fact remains that Hildegard was a twelfth-century woman. She lived in a pre-modern, pre-Freudian age, and while her incredible gifts and her remarkable legacy make her resonant to us today, to do her justice we need to meet Hildegard in her own world, to hear her own voice.

Reading historical texts is an exercise in dialogue and reflection. In doing so, we are encountering a person from another age who nonetheless lived a human life, similar to ours in some ways, but in other ways different. In reading historical texts, we communicate with the wider human community across the span of thousands of years. Many of these historical figures also read and reflected on texts in their era. The points below help frame the reading of Hildegard's texts in a way that values her voice, her humanity, and the spirit in which she wrote them.

We read texts such as Hildegard's because they illuminate our own experiences; in appreciating Hildegard's words, we can develop our own insights and our own spirits. At the same time, we have to be careful not to project our own agendas onto Hildegard's texts. Her experiences were her own, just as ours belong to us. Whether you sit down and read Hildegard's texts in one sitting or reflect on a few at one time, try to keep the following points in mind. Take the time to engage in a dialogue with and to reflect on the text before you rush to a conclusion. Over time these methods will be incorporated into your own way of "seeing" the text.

- Always remember that history is not progressive; we in the twenty-first century are not necessarily more enlightened, sensitive, or in touch with the yearnings of the human heart than Hildegard and her contemporaries were. Quite the contrary, we share in a common humanity, and have many of the same deep needs, though our ways of seeing our place in the world (our worldview) and communicating who we are and what we are all about have changed over time.
- Begin by reading through each text one time in its entirety. Read with compassion and respect for the author; try to suspend prejudices and judgments. The story of Hildegard of Bingen is but one illustration of the creative and fulfilling lives of people who lived in the Middle Ages. If someone one hundred years from now read a text that you had written, how would you like to be regarded as the author?
- Read the text in context. Consider the people, places, time, and other identifying information. What do you know about Hildegard

that informs your reading of the text? Is there a particular location that is important? Which community or communities is Hildegard addressing? Sometimes she is addressing her nuns; sometimes she is writing to a political ruler; sometimes she is writing to a religious leader.

- What is Hildegard's thesis or argument? Why is she writing this text? Try to identify the key issue or theme the text is addressing and put it in your own words.

- Consider the literary characteristics of the text. What kind of text is it—hymn, letter, homily, poem, part of a book? Is this the whole text or part of a larger text? Are there words, patterns, themes, images, and metaphors that keep emerging? What are Hildegard's sources? Is she quoting from Scripture or another work?

- Allow yourself to be transported to the author's context and experience. Read deeply and allow Hildegard's voice to emerge. What is she saying to you, now? How have you been changed by this text?

- What questions remain? Are there questions you would like to ask Hildegard, if you had the chance?

- Think about applying the text. Are there ways this text relates to people today? Are there ways in which you feel drawn to interpret this text through the creative arts—drama, song, drawing, painting, photography?

Of course, to make medieval texts accessible, we need to apply the author's words to contemporary life. But it is also important not to rush into application. Rather, challenge yourself to listen to Hildegard's voice as it emerges from the texts. As St. Benedict taught, we need to learn to "listen with the ear of our hearts." To understand and experience Hildegard's texts we must first relate to them from her own perspective before we make interpretations based solely on our own experience. Not only do we have to bring our minds and gifts of analysis to the texts, but we must also bring our hearts and our spirits. Hildegard was taught to listen with the ear of her heart from the time she was a small child. Her texts resonate on many levels because she brought her whole self to her work. Only when we make an effort to understand Hildegard's life and works in her own context can we begin the dialogue between the two worlds—the world of a twelfth-century mystic and our own.

Encountering Hildegard's Music

Many people have their first encounter with Hildegard of Bingen through her music. Since the early 1980s various musicians and vocal ensembles have recorded Hildegard's compositions, and her complete musical works are now available. Music was at the heart of Hildegard's creativity, and she refers to music over three hundred times in her theological, philosophical, and scientific writings. As concert pianist and lecturer Nancy Fierro, CSJ, notes:

> For Hildegard, music was an all-embracing concept. It was the symphony of angels praising God, the balanced proportions of the revolving celestial spheres, the exquisite weaving of body and soul, the hidden design of nature's creations. It was the manifest process of life moving, expanding, growing towards the joy of its own deepest realizations and a profound unity of voices singing the praises of God here on earth. It was beauty, sound, fragrance and the flower of human artistry.[61]

Hildegard's music was derived from plainsong chants, the earliest Christian chants, which evolved from Jewish chants. Pope Gregory I (590–604) preserved and notated them. Gregory referred to chant as the "song of the angels," and was said to have received the gift of chant from a dove, or the Holy Spirit, who came to sit on his shoulder and sing in his ear.[62] Chanting is one of the most ancient spiritual practices, known not only by Jews and Christians, but also found in Hindu, Buddhist, Taoist, and other spiritual traditions. For thousands of years human beings have believed that chanting carries with it divine power, and that as a spiritual practice it transforms the soul, mind, and body. Health studies have found that listening to chant can "lower blood pressure, increase levels of DHEA, and also reduce anxiety and depression."[63] Though Hildegard's composi-tions were clearly grounded in her religious tradition, to appreciate her music we need not be limited to one tradition or belief system. Rather, the evocative quality of her music, like the rhythm of a heartbeat, can bring with it spiritual, mental, and physical benefits, as well as fostering peace within ourselves and the world around us.

Hildegard's monastery was an ideal environment for a composer, in that it had a skilled group of nuns to sing the music, a liturgical calendar that framed the occasions for performance, and a scriptorium with skilled copyists who could pen the music. When Hildegard was composing, notation was only a little over a century old, and melody was a single line sung by a soloist or a choir. Although traditionally no instruments were used to accompany plainchant, Hildegard may have used instruments. Whether she used them or not in her own monastery, she affirmed the use of instruments in general as a way to soften the heart and direct it toward God. She also believed that certain instruments had special sig-nificance. For instance, a flute reminds us of the breath of the Spirit; the strings stir the heart and call the soul back to repentance; and the harp recalls our origins and reminds us of heaven.[64]

Many find Hildegard's compositions exceedingly evocative. For those interested in experiencing Hildegard's music, it is important to fully listen to the Latin chant to appreciate the rhythms of the words and melody, whether or not the language is literally understood. The words and music work together to convey emotions so powerful that it is not necessary to understand the Latin to be profoundly touched. The listener is aided by first listening and experiencing them in the language in which they were composed, and then, as a later step, tackling a translation of the lyrics. Some find it efficacious to listen to Hildegard's compositions as a form of meditation or prayer. Others play the music at work or while driving to reduce stress and to calm down. Still others play Hildegard's music at home for their family or to soothe small children. Even pets have been known to be calmed by the sound of chant.

Hildegard was a dramatic artist. Her artistry appeals to all the senses—deep colors, fragrant scents, evocative sounds. The intensity of her compositions is reflected in both the words and the sounds. In contrast to other chants of her day, Hildegard's music has a very wide vocal range. According to musicologist Marianne Pfau, Hildegard uses extremes of register to create the "soaring arches" that are characteristic of her music and are reminiscent of bringing heaven and earth together.[65] Hildegard's style is also distinguished by large leaps up and down the scale and melodies with rapid ascents and slow declines. In her compositions she seeks to bring together the heart, mind, and body while celebrating celestial harmony in heaven and on earth.[66]

Hildegard's words and music reach across the years to enrich hearts, minds, and spirits today. Her texts deserve to be read and reread to discern Hildegard's wisdom and message for contemporary readers. Her music can transport the listener to the gates of paradise. This book provides a glimpse into the multifaceted world of Hildegard of Bingen. May you be blessed with many years of her companionship along the way.

Part 1
Living Light

From the time she was a little girl, Hildegard had mystical experiences "bathed in light." In her visions, day or night, she experienced this non-spatial light, which she referred to as the reflection of the "Living Light," meaning God. It might not be possible to always see the complete radiance of God, but it is possible to see the reflection or shadow of that radiance every day. Hildegard's mystical gifts enabled her to see daily events with the depths of her soul, constantly, to such an extent that it was debilitating to her health. At the same time, the Living Light, which came to her when she was fully awake and sometimes spoke to her in Latin, brought to her the powerful images that she was commanded to write down for others.

1 Antiphons are responsive chants sung before and after psalms or the Magnificat during matins or vespers in the Divine Office. Hildegard's antiphons tended to be longer than customary. In regard to angels, she believed in a heavenly hierarchy whereby all the angels, saints, human beings, and animals had their part in praising God. The nine orders of angels came just after God the Father, Jesus Christ, and the Virgin Mary in order of precedence, and just before the categories of saints. Hildegard saw angels as forms of complete light and perfect beauty whose main task is to ever praise God. Collectively, the angels reflect the Living Light and are a glimpse of the soul's desire.

2 The "fallen angel" here refers to the Devil, once close to God, but ruined by his desire to be higher than God.

3 The use of *fall* refers to the fallen angel from the Garden of Eden who persuaded Adam and Eve to sin, thereby afflicting all of creation.

4 In this excerpt from the introduction of the *Scivias,* Hildegard writes of the history of her visions, experienced as brilliant light flowing through her body. She mentions that she had the visions from the age of five. Elsewhere she writes of having visions as early as the age of three. Either way, the visions of light were with her from her earliest memories.

☐ Antiphon for the Angels

O most glorious angels of Living Light,
Who, beneath divinity, gaze on the eyes of God
within the mysterious darkness of every created thing,
in ardent desires
so you will never be satiated.[1]
O how glorious are the joys
of your being,
that is untouched
by every evil work,
that had their beginnings,
in the fallen angel[2]
who sought to fly
higher than the hidden pinnacle of God,
so he plummeted down in ruin.
This fall serves as a warning[3]
to all created by God's finger.

SYMPHONIA (SONGS) 29

☐ The Living Light Since Childhood

In the year 1141 of the incarnation of God's Son, Jesus Christ, when I
was forty-two years and seven months old, the heavens were opened
and a blinding light of exceptional brilliance flowed through my whole
brain.[4] Like a flame it kindled my whole heart and my breast, not burning but warming, as the sun warms anything on which its rays fall.
Suddenly I understood the meanings of Scripture—the Psalter, the Gospels, and other catholic books of the Old and New Testaments—not,

(continued on page 5)

5 | As a woman in a patriarchal church and culture, Hildegard was very careful, at least until the end of her life, to always claim the divine origins of any knowledge, lest she incur punishment for herself and her community. Here she explains how the Living Light, or God, inspired her with knowledge of the Scriptures. Certainly, she also was more learned than most women in this regard, yet she was cautious to claim such knowledge for herself.

6 | Unlike other mystics, Hildegard experienced her visions while fully awake, and not in a trance or ecstatic state.

7 | Hildegard insists on the Divine as the origin of her visions. Her enlightenment is because of the Living Light, not due to formal training.

8 | Shortly before her scribe Gottfried of Disibodenberg died in 1174 or 1175, Hildegard began a correspondence with the monk Guibert of Gembloux, who lived in what is now Belgium. He was very learned in Latin literature, and edited *Solutions to Thirty-Eight Questions* with the monks of the monastery of Villers and sent the manuscript to

however, that I understood the words of the text or how to divide them into syllables or their cases and tenses.[5]

This mysterious power of secret and wonderful visions I have sensed in myself since childhood—from the time that I was five years old—up to the present time. But I revealed it to no one but the religious who lived in my community. Up until the time that God in his grace wished it to be revealed, I have quietly repressed it in silence.

The visions that I see I perceive not in dreams and not while asleep; not in ecstasy and not with my bodily eyes or external ears; I do not see them in hidden places, but I behold them openly, awake and alert, purely with the eyes and ears of a clear mind, according to the will of God. How this may be is difficult for mortals to comprehend.[6]

INTRODUCTION, *SCIVIAS* (KNOW THE WAYS OF THE LORD)

□ The Reflection of the Living Light

How could God work through me if I were not aware that I am a poor creature? God works where he will for the glory of his name, and not for that of an earthly person. I have always had a trembling fear, since I have never felt secure in my own capacities. But I stretch out my hands to God, like a feather that lacks all weight and flies on the wind.[7] I cannot know perfectly the things that I see while I am in my bodily form with an invisible spirit, since humanity is lacking in these two things.

From my early childhood, before my bones, nerves, and veins were fully strengthened, I have always seen this vision in my soul, even to the present time, when I am more than seventy years old....[8] The light that I see thus is not confined in one place, but it is far, far brighter than a cloud that carries the sun; nor can I ascertain its height or length or breadth.... And I call it "the reflection of the Living Light." Just as the sun and the moon and the stars appear in the waters, so the Scriptures,

(continued on page 7)

Hildegard in 1176. From 1177 he was her secretary, and served her devotedly until her death in 1179. In 1180 he returned to Gembloux. He was elected abbot of Florennes in Namur in 1188 or 1189 and abbot of Gembloux in 1194. Guibert's letters to Hildegard were long and insistent. Despite the fact that Hildegard was in her late seventies, Guibert had very high expectations about the level of detail he expected in Hildegard's responses, and he was disappointed if she did not answer him right away. Perhaps she grew weary of his attentions? If he did not get an answer when expected, he wrote her again, asking more questions. Still, he praises her lavishly, saying she is equal to the great women prophets of the Hebrew Bible, and she is unparalleled among women, with the exception of the Blessed Virgin.

In this portion of a letter to Guibert, written as Hildegard is nearing the end of her life, she explains her visions as "the reflection of the Living Light."

9 | In this section of the letter, which occurs about halfway through the text, and after a more theological section, Hildegard explains her visions and repeats the image she uses frequently of herself as a feather carried on the wind, or a feather on the breath of God.

10 | Hildegard always insists that she receives her visions while fully awake, and not in an ecstatic trance.

11 | Hildegard explains the source of her extensive knowledge as a reflection of her visions. From this section of the letter we obtain a glimpse of Hildegard's writing process, as well as her prodigious memory.

sermons, and virtues, and certain works that humans have wrought, shine on me brightly in this light. Whatever I see or learn in this vision, I hold in my memory a long time; so I see, hear, and know all at once, and, as if in an instant, I learn what I know. But what I do not see, I do not know, for I am not educated, but I have simply been taught how to read. And what I write is what I hear and I see in the vision.... And the words in this vision are not like words uttered by the mouth of a man, but like a shimmering flame, or a cloud floating in a clear sky.[9]

The light I see is not local and confined. It is much brighter than the cloud that surrounds the sun. I can discern neither its height nor its length and breadth. This light I named the "shadow of the Living Light," and just as the sun, moon, and stars appear reflected in water, so too are the Scriptures, sermons, virtues, and deeds of humanity reflected back to me from it.[10]

I retain the memory of whatever I see or learn in a vision for a long time, and so I remember it. What I see and hear and know are simultaneously one, so that I learn and know in an instant. But what I do not see there, I do not know, since I am unlearned. The things that I write, I see and hear in my vision, and I do not put down any other words of my own. I express whatever I hear in the vision in unpolished Latin, since I have not been taught to write as philosophers do. Moreover, the words that I see and hear in the vision are not like the words of human speech, but like a blazing flame and a cloud that moved through clear air. I cannot in any way ascertain the form of this light, just as I cannot stare fully into the sun.[11]

Occasionally, though not often, I see another light in that light, which I have called the "Living Light." But I am even less able to explain this light than I can the first one. Yet when I behold it, all sadness and all pain vanish from my memory and I feel more like a carefree young girl than the old woman that I am.

To Guibert of Gembloux, 1175; *Epistolarium* (Letters) 103R

~ This amazing passage is taken from the *Scivias* and relates to Hildegard's second vision, which focuses on the Trinity. In it she not only uses her image of the Living Light, but she also brings in another favorite image, fire. Rather than a Trinity with sharp boundaries between the Father, the Son, and the Holy Spirit, Hildegard's Trinity is one of dynamic relationship and inclusion. The three persons of the Trinity are inextricably and forever inseparable. The vision of the Trinity is prefaced by a vision of a sapphire Jesus Christ, whereby the Living Light explains the mystery of the Trinity to Hildegard. This vision is often depicted as circles of light and fire—some suggest reminiscent of the womb—surrounding the sapphire figure of Christ. The image resembles an eye, symbolizing the way the Father and the Holy Spirit gaze on humanity through Jesus.

12 The three persons of the Trinity are represented by the Father, or the light of God; the Holy Spirit, or the fire; both are poured out in the human figure who receives both the light and the fire, the Son. Jesus Christ is related to both the light of the Father and the fire of the Holy Spirit.

13 The theme of the "eternal begetting" of the Son is also in Hildegard's other works, and refers to the Athanasian Creed, a Christian statement of belief in use since the sixth century. This creed focuses on the themes of the Trinity and the nature of Christ. It was the first creed in which the equality of all three persons of the Trinity—Father, Son, and Holy Spirit—is explicitly stated.

14 These are various interpretations of the use of the color sapphire, or blue, to depict Jesus Christ. One is that blue is reminiscent of water, and baptism, and the symbolism of Jesus who washed away all sin.

☐ The Trinity

And again I heard the Living Light, say to me: Therefore you see "an extremely bright light," which signifies the Father, who is without the stains of illusion, failure, or deceit. And in the light is "the figure of a man the color of sapphire," which represents the Son, who is without the stains of hardheartedness, envy, or evil, and who before time began, was begotten of the Father in divinity, but afterwards became incarnate in the world in humanity. And "it was all burning in a delightful red fire." This is the fire without flaws of aridity, mortality, or darkness, which represents the Holy Spirit, by whom the Only Begotten Son of the Father was conceived in the flesh, born of the Virgin and poured out his light and truth over all the world.[12] And the bright light flooded through all the glowing fire, and the glowing fire bathed all the bright light and the glowing fire shone over the whole figure of the man so that the three were one light in strength and power.

This means that the Father, who is Justice, is not without the Son or the Holy Spirit, and that the Holy Spirit, who inflames the hearts of the faithful, is not without the Father or the Son, nor the Son without the Father, nor the Father or the Son without the Holy Spirit, nor the Spirit without them. Thus these three persons exist as one God in one perfect divine majesty, and the unity of their divinity is inseparable, because divinity cannot be separated, since it always remains unchanged without any mutability. But the Father is revealed through the Son, the Son through creation, and the Holy Spirit through the incarnate Son. How is this? It is the Father who begot the Son before all ages;[13] it is the Son through whom all things were made by the Father at the beginning of creation; and it is the Holy Spirit who appeared in the form of a dove at the baptism[14] of the Son of God before the end of all time.

SCIVIAS (KNOW THE WAYS OF THE LORD) 2.2

15   Hildegard's reference to "fragile vessels" is taken from 2 Corinthians 4:6–7: "For God, who commanded the light to shine out of darkness, hath shined in our hearts, to give the light of the knowledge of the glory of God in the face of Jesus Christ. But we have this treasure in earthen vessels, that the excellency of the power may be of God, and not of us."

16   In Hildegard's cosmology, humanity is the highest level of creation, and God created all to serve humanity.

17   This text is from a letter to Elisabeth of Schönau (1126–1165), who was, like Hildegard, a Benedictine visionary and mystic, and the histories of the two women are related. Hildegard even sent a manuscript containing some of her works and Elisabeth's to the Cistercian monastery of Villers. Elisabeth lived in the double monastery of Schönau in Nassau. Though Elizabeth was influenced by the more senior and more widely known Hildegard, her visions and works differ from Hildegard's in significant ways. Elisabeth's visions began in 1152 and generally occurred on Sundays and Holy Days. She dictated in German to her brother, a priest, who then translated her narratives into Latin. Her visions occurred while she was in a trance, and do not indicate the same level of familiarity with Scripture and other theological works that Hildegard's do. At first Elisabeth's apocalyptic prophecies were not that well received, but her later visions authenticating relics, like those of St. Ursula, were popular. Like Hildegard, Elisabeth also suffered from debilitating illnesses; however, unlike Hildegard, Elisabeth's are attributed to her strict asceticism—practices that were condemned by the older nun, who urged her protégée to take care of the "fragile vessel" of her body. The letters between the two women are important because they show Hildegard in her mentoring and spiritual director's role with a younger visionary of wide acclaim. Hildegard was one of the few at the time who was in a position to guide Elisabeth. In this letter she advises Elisabeth that, indeed, the Devil does pay attention to those who have a special relationship with the Living Light. In a touching way, Hildegard assures Elisabeth that she, too, gets overwhelmed,

☐ Spiritual Guidance to Another Woman Mystic

I, a poor little woman and a fragile vessel[15] say these things not from myself but from the Serene Light: Humanity is a vessel that God fashioned for himself, and which he filled with his inspiration, so he may perfect his works in him. For God does not work as humankind does, but so that all things may be perfected according to his commands. The plants, the forests, and the trees appeared, the sun also, the moon and the stars came forth, to support humanity. The waters brought forth fish and birds, cattle and beasts, which all serve humankind as appointed by God.[16]

All acknowledged God, except human beings alone. For they turned away from God, and elevated themselves, although God gave them knowledge. God intended to perfect his works in human beings, but the Devil deceived them, through an unreasonable wind, when they sought out more than they should have, and tainted them with the sin of disobedience.[17]

(continued on page 13)

but yet she receives comfort from the Living Light, which supports her in God's service. Overall, the letter relates a positive perspective, for its day, on the creation of the world and God's action in human history.

18 This refers to the story of Cain and Abel in Genesis 4:2–16. Cain and Abel were two sons of Adam and Eve; Abel was committed to following God's commands, and so favored by God. He was consequently murdered in a jealous rage by Cain. Despite human tendencies to disobey God, there were some humans, like Abel, whom God aided because of their goodness.

19 From Psalm 45:2: "Thou art fairer than the children of men: grace is poured into thy lips: therefore God hath blessed thee forever."

20 Adapted from Malachi 4:2: "But unto you that fear my name shall the Sun of Righteousness arise with healing in his wings; and ye shall go forth, and grow up as calves of the stall."

21 Benedictines were very conscious of time, and divided the day into canonical hours, when they gathered in chapel, the sixth hour being noon. However, Hildegard may also be referring to the text of Matthew 27:45–46, which speaks of the sixth hour as the time of the crucifixion.

22 Hildegard's advice is to be vigilant because the Devil takes particular interest in those with visionary gifts. The reference to the clouds is from Isaiah 14:12–15: "How art thou fallen from heaven, O Lucifer, son of the morning! How art thou cut down to the ground, which didst weaken the nations! For thou hast said in thine heart, I will ascend into heaven, I will exalt my throne above the stars of God: I will sit also upon the mount of the congregation, in the sides of the north: I will ascend above the heights of the clouds; I will be like the most High. Yet thou shalt be brought down to hell, to the sides of the pit."

Ach! Woe! Then all the elements enfolded themselves in the alteration of light and shadows, just as humankind did by transgressing God's commands. But God succored certain people so that humanity would not be totally mocked. For Abel was a good man, but Cain was a murderer.[18] And many saw the mysteries of God in the light, but others committed many sins, until the time came when God's Word shone forth, as was said: "Thou are beautiful above the children of men."[19] Then the Sun of Justice[20] illuminated humanity with good works in faith and deed, just as the dawn comes first and the rest of the hours fall until night comes. So, O my anxious daughter Elisabeth, the world is changed. For now the world has run through the time of cultivating values, that is, the dawn, the first, the third, and the sixth—the most vital hour of the day.[21] But in this time it is necessary for God to succor other people, lest his instruments become useless.

Listen, O anxious daughter, that the ambitious suggestion of the ancient serpent sometimes wearies those people who are filled with the inspiration of God. For whenever the serpent sees a beautiful gem, he hisses, saying: "What is this?" He harasses such people with many miseries as the blazing mind desires to soar above the clouds, like gods, just as he himself once did.[22]

Listen again: Those who long to perform God's works should always remember that, being human, they are fragile vessels. Always bear in mind what they are and what they will be. They must leave the heavenly things to him who is of heaven, for they are exiles, ignorant of heavenly things. They can only sing the mysteries of God like a trumpet, which of itself gives no sound, except when another breathes into it that it may give forth a sound. But those who are mild, gentle, poor, and afflicted, just like the Lamb, should put on the breastplate of faith. For they are the sound of his trumpet, they are as innocent children. For

(continued on page 15)

23 Here Hildegard comments on how God "chastises" or brings suffering to those who are closest to him, yet never to the point of perishing.

24 On a personal note, Hildegard shares that she, too grows weary from time to time, but through the Living Light she is able to remain of service. She hopes that Elisabeth will continue to reflect God's holiness in her life.

25 In Hildegard's writings, as in Scripture, mountains and mountaintops are associated with salvation.

26 This text is an excerpt from a letter to Henry (Heinrich) of Liège, a major church figure during Hildegard's era, as well as a favorite of Emperor Frederick Barbarossa. He was one of the supporters of Hildegard's monastery at Rupertsberg. He also supported the emperor in his conflicts with two popes, Adrian IV and Alexander III, and helped consecrate one antipope. This letter is a response to a letter in which he implored Hildegard to pray for him, in certain knowledge that God would indeed listen to her prayers. Her response is to lament the slothfulness and sin in the world, and to remind him of his obligation to bring back those who have drifted away from the church. This letter is an example of how even highly placed church officials had confidence in Hildegard's visions and holiness.

In this image of the Living Light, Hildegard shares her vision of the path of the Scriptures to the holy mountain, and the day that Christ came into the world.

27 In this section Hildegard compares the difficult times in the church of her day with a mountain covered with a cloud so dense that it no longer emits a sweet fragrance. Hildegard tells Henry that he must be a good pastor to restore the church to its former standing and to gain God's favor for himself.

God always chastises those who sound his trumpet, but according to his own good purpose, he foresees that their fragile vessel will not perish.[23]

O my daughter, may God make you the mirror of life. I too am downcast in my wavering mind, and am greatly troubled with anxiety and fears. Yet from time to time I resound like the small blast of a trumpet from the Living Light. May God help me to remain in his service.[24]

To Elisabeth of Schönau, ca. 1152–1156; *Epistolarium* (Letters) 201R

☐ The Path of the Scriptures

The Living Light says the path of the Scriptures leads directly to the high mountain,[25] where the flowers and aromatic herbs grow; where a pleasant wind blows, bringing forth their powerful aroma; where the roses and the lilies reveal their shining faces. But because of the shadows of the dark living air, that mountain of the most high did not appear until the Son that enlightened the world. On that day, the sun rose from the dawn, illuminating this world so that all people could see its aromatic herbs. That day was very beautiful and good news came into the world.[26]

But O shepherds, now is the time for mourning and weeping, because in our time the mountain has been covered with a very black cloud so that it no longer sends forth its gentle fragrance. You, Henry, must be a good shepherd, noble of character. And just as the eagle gazes into the sun, consider how you can restore the slothful and the prodigal to their homeland, and how you can restore some light to this mountain, so that your soul may live. Thus you will hear the voice of the most loving Judge on high: "Well done, good and faithful servant." Then your soul will shine like a soldier brilliant in the light, who rejoices with his comrades because he has gained the victory.[27]

(continued on page 17)

28 At the end of the letter, Hildegard reminds Henry of his duty to cleanse the church of error and prepare the people for Christ's return.

29 The phrase "poor little woman" is one of many phrases that Hildegard uses to describe herself throughout her writings. Similar phrases are used by other women mystics, and have less to say about the women's self-image than they do about the belief that it is God, and not their own abilities, who is responsible for their mystical inspirations.

30 This letter was written by Hildegard to Pope Eugenius (Eugene) III shortly after the Synod of Trier and before she completed the *Scivias* in 1151. It is also one of the earliest letters written by Hildegard that we have. Eugenius, the first Cistercian pope, was known as a mild and spiritual ruler. He was pope when few other men sought the office, given that the papacy was vulnerable to attacks from within and from outside. As a close friend of the reformer Bernard of Clairvaux, he was considered an acceptable candidate. Eugenius was committed to reform of the clergy, but was unable to spend much of his pontificate in Rome due to danger and unrest. In this letter, Hildegard writes to the pope on her own behalf, hoping for his support of her writing down her visions.

31 Hildegard stresses that the Light that is guiding her writing has been with her for many years. It is not uncommon to find that mystics keep their visions secret for many years before they are shared.

Therefore, teacher of the people, fight for the victory. Correct those in error, and wash the mud from the beautiful pearls. Prepare them for the Most High King. Let your mind sigh with eagerness to bring those pearls to the mountain where the gift of God had originally planted them. May God protect you now, and free your soul from eternal punishment.[28]

To Henry, Bishop of Liège, ca. 1148–1153; *Epistolarium* (Letters) 37R

☐ A Request for the Pope's Support

Gentle father, poor little woman that I am,[29] I write to you now those things that God wishes me to teach in a true vision, by mystical inspiration.[30]

Radiant father, through your representatives you came to us in your official capacity, as God willed it, and you have seen something of the true visions that the Living Light has taught me, and you heard them in the embrace of your heart. Now that a part of this writing is finished, the same Light has not left me but burns in my soul as it has since childhood.[31] Therefore I now send you this letter as God has instructed me. And my spirit desires that the light from the Light shine within you and purify your eyes and awaken your spirit to these writings, so that your soul may be crowned, as God so wishes. But many wise men

(continued on page 19)

32   Hildegard states that she is coming to him because she has been criticized for writing down her visions, but, she stresses, she writes them under God's instructions, not because she has academic training. The phrase "poor female figure formed in the rib" refers to Eve, who came from Adam's rib, and popular references to women as the "daughter of Eve" in medieval sources.

33   This is the first extant example of Hildegard's usage of the image of herself as a feather on the breath of God.

34   Hildegard reminds Eugenius, in not-so-humble fashion this time, that her visions are indeed from God, and that God bids him to approve her writing, which is a source of revelation.

of earthly inclinations have rejected these writings of mine, criticizing me, this poor female figure formed in the rib and not taught by the philosophers.[32]

Father of pilgrims, hear the voice of him who is: A mighty king sat in his hall, high pillars before him covered in gold bands and adorned with pearls and precious stones. It pleased this king to touch a tiny feather, so that it soared up miraculously, and a strong wind bore it up so that it did not fall.[33]

He who is the Living Light shining in the heavens and in the abyss, and who lies hidden in the listening hearts, now says to you: Prepare this writing to be received by those who hear me; make it fruitful with the juice of sweetness; make it a root of the branches, and a soaring leaf in the face of the Devil. Then you will have eternal life. Do not reject these mysteries of God, for they are part of that which is hidden and which has not been revealed.[34]

May the sweetest fragrance be in you. May you never grow weary on the path of justice.

TO POPE EUGENIUS III, 1148; *EPISTOLARIUM* (LETTERS) 2

Part 2
Blazing Fire

Throughout her texts, Hildegard makes expansive use of traditional biblical imagery in describing the work of the Holy Spirit as a "blazing fire,"
characterized by heat, warmth, and an eternal flame. Hildegard's "blazing
fire" is a life force, a fiery divine energy that enflames humanity and permeates the entire cosmos. She also writes of the life-giving Spirit as the
"fire of creation," along with wisdom and love. Many of the images of
Hildegard's visionary texts are filled with references to the elements—fire,
earth, air, and water—that lie at the very center of human life. Human
beings are both inspired and sustained by fire.

〰️ This text is from a letter from Hildegard to Bernard of Clairvaux (1090–1153), the most important Cistercian of his time, and a widely respected abbot and theological writer. Through his intervention, Hildegard's writings were accepted at the Synod of Trier, 1147–1148. This is the first extant letter we have from Hildegard, and it was written at the time when she was preparing to share her visions with a wider audience. Hildegard wanted the church to officially sanction her visions, so Bernard was a natural choice for Hildegard's correspondence. Though his response was brief and unemotional, given the intense tone of Hildegard's request, she did receive the support from him that she needed: Bernard acknowledged that her visions were indeed from God.

Renowned Hildegard scholar Beverly Mayne Kienzle writes that Bernard's answer to Hildegard, affirming her gift from the Holy Spirit, was a paraphrase of 1 John 2:27: "But the anointing which ye have received of him abideth in you, and ye need not that any man teach you: but as the same anointing teacheth you of all things, and is truth, and is no lie, and even as it hath taught you, ye shall abide in him." (See Kienzle, *Hildegard of Bingen: Homilies on the Gospels* [Collegeville, MN: Liturgical Press, 2011], 20–21.)

It is commonly believed that Bernard showed Hildegard's letter to the pope, who was also at the synod. The pope then asked for the entire manuscript, and read it to the assembled prelates, who unanimously agreed that Hildegard should be encouraged in her writing. This excerpt centers on Hildegard's request to Bernard.

1 This refers to Bernard's preaching about the Second Crusade, 1146–1147.

2 Here Hildegard explains how long she has been having her visions, and the stress she has lived under since her childhood in keeping silent about them. Hildegard's claims of her "wretchedness" as a woman are likely an effort to establish the divine nature of her visions.

☐ Hildegard Describes Her Visions to Bernard of Clairvaux

Venerable Father Bernard, you are highly honored by God. You bring fear to the unlawful foolishness of the world; and in your intense zeal you burn in the love of God's Son; you gather men into Christ's army for the banner of the cross against pagan savagery.[1] I ask you, in the name of the living God, to answer my questions.

Father, I am most troubled about this vision, which appeared to me through divine revelation, and which I never saw with the eyes of the flesh, but only with my spirit. Wretched, and more than wretched in that I bear the name of woman, and I have from earliest childhood seen great miracles, which my tongue could not describe, had not the spirit of God taught me that I may believe.

Most steadfast and gentle Father, reply in your goodness to me, your unworthy servant, for from my infancy I have never lived one hour free from anxiety. In your piety and wisdom, consult your soul, as you have been taught by the Holy Spirit, and grant heartfelt consolation to your handmaid.[2]

(continued on page 25)

3 Hildegard's visions touch her like a burning flame, with a deep understanding of Scripture, despite her lack of formal theological training. This kind of training would not have been available to a woman at that time, though it has been established that Hildegard was well educated. Beverly Mayne Kienzle points out that monastic exegesis of the era tended to stress the spiritual rather than the literal meaning of the text (*Homilies on the Gospels,* 8). Also, at this point in her life, Hildegard was less intellectually assertive than in her later years. She wants to make clear that her visions, which come when she is awake, are directly from God.

4 This monk is Volmar of Disibodenberg.

5 There were many heretical sects in the twelfth century, and Hildegard no doubt heard of them and wanted to make sure to distance herself from them. Her concern was always to establish her orthodoxy. During the period of the letter, the pope actually sent Bernard to France to deal with troublesome heretics.

6 In the closing paragraph in this section of the letter, Hildegard states that she hopes she will receive word from Bernard as to whether she should speak about her visions or continue to remain silent, though there is a connection between being silent and her infirmities. Throughout her life, whenever Hildegard's prophetic voice was silenced, her illnesses came back.

Through this vision, which touches my heart and soul like a burning flame, teaching me such profundities of exposition, I know the inner meaning of the Psalms, the Gospels, and the other volumes, which are shown to me in this vision. But I do not receive this expertise in German. Because I am a person without formal training, I only know how to read simply, and not with a deep analysis. But I seek your response to this matter, because I am only taught inwardly, from my soul. That is why I speak in doubt.[3]

But when I hear your wisdom and piety I will be comforted. I have not dared to tell these things to anyone, except a certain monk[4] whom I have observed to be more upright than the rest, since there are so many heresies abroad,[5] as I have heard. I have revealed all my secrets to this man, and he has indeed supported me, for these are great and fearsome matters.

For the love of God, I wish that you might console me, Father, that I will be reassured. More than two years ago, I saw you in a vision, like a man gazing straight into the sun, completely unafraid. And I wept because I am so ashamed and fearful. Good and most gentle Father, I have been placed in your care, so you can reveal to me through our correspondence whether you wish me to speak openly or keep my silence, because I have great anxiety about this visionary gift with respect to how much I should speak about what I have seen and heard. Meanwhile, I have been laid low, bedridden by great infirmities, and unable to raise myself up.[6]

To Bernard of Clairvaux, ca. 1146–1147; *Epistolarium* (Letters) 1

7 In this rendition of the Trinity, Hildegard uses images of the three qualities of the godhead seen in the unity of one flame. All three persons are necessary, unified, and yet distinct. The images of light, fire, and flame are those used to signify the soul's transformation and union with God. Interestingly, none of the images themselves are gender-specific, suggesting a vision of the Trinity that goes beyond traditional categories.

8 Here is an example of the way Hildegard often prefaced her visions. That is, she explains that she is a poor, uneducated woman, as a sign of humility, and probably as a way to protect herself from claims that she was acting irresponsibly or beyond her station. The "weaker rib" is a reference to Eve, the mother of all, who came from Adam's rib.

9 This, the introduction to a vision in *Scivias*, is included here because of Hildegard's reference to fire in several ways—as knowledge, as mystical inspiration, and as the fire of divine love that lives within.

Hildegard claims her mystical visions are the most radiant fire. Though humble about her lack of formal education, she insists on the divine origin of her mystical experiences.

☐ Three Powers in the Glowing Heat of a Flame

Just as there are three qualities in the heat of a flame, so the one God is in three persons.[7] How so? The flame consists of radiant light, red vitality, and fiery heat. It has a radiant light so that it may shine in its light, and red vigor so that it can endure, and a fiery heat so that it can burn. Consider the Father in the brilliant light, for he sends out his brightness to the faithful through the goodness of his fatherhood. In the red vitality held within the flame and containing its strength, think of the Son, who was born from the Virgin, in which the divine wonders are shown. In the fiery heat perceive the Holy Spirit, who burns fire in the minds of believers. For the flame will not be seen if there is no radiant light or red vitality or fiery heat. In the same way, God is not honored in any place where neither the Father, the Son, nor the Holy Spirit is worshipped.

Therefore as these three persons are discerned in the one flame, so three persons must be understood in the unity of the divinity.

SCIVIAS (KNOW THE WAYS OF THE LORD) 11.2.6

☐ Fire like the Burning Sun

And I—a human being ablaze
with neither the strength of strong lions
nor education in their exhalations,
limited by the fragility of the weaker rib[8]
but flooded with mystical inspiration
saw the most radiant fire,
unfathomable, inextinguishable,
fully alive and filled with life,
with a flame the color of air.[9]

(continued on page 29)

10 In this text, Hildegard compares the will to a fire that bakes human actions in an oven, like bread, so that people will be nourished and live better lives. Like Augustine and Bernard of Clairvaux, Hildegard asserts that moral agency requires human beings to perform their actions freely by virtue of the will. According to Hildegard, the will activates the work; the intellect receives it; and reason produces it.

The will and the intellect are connected; only those who have a mature intellect are capable of acting freely. For the intellect knows good and evil. Therefore, the work of the will is different at various times in the life cycle. Nevertheless, the intellect is merely an instrument by which the will is able to exercise choice. The will depends on the intellect to identify what choices are available; people cannot choose what they are not aware of. Once the intellect has revealed possible alternatives for action, its job is finished. The will makes the final choice of what is to be done.

And I heard a voice from that living fire speaking to me:
Forlorn earthly creature!
As a woman
you are unlearned in any of the teachings
of human masters
that is, unable to read
with the understanding of the philosophers,
nevertheless, you are embraced by my light,
which touches your innermost being
with fire like the burning sun.
Shout, and tell, and write down
these, my mysteries,
which you see and hear in this mystical vision.

Scivias (Know the Ways of the Lord) 2.1

☐ Fire and Bread

The will is like a fire baking every action in an oven. Bread is baked in order to nourish people so they may live. Thus, the will is the force behind the whole of work. It grinds our work in a mill, it adds yeast and kneads it vigorously, and thus prepares the work in contemplation, like a loaf of bread that the will bakes to perfection by its ardor. In so doing it gives human beings a better food than the bread they eat. For while the human body stops eating from time to time, the work of the will endures within the human being until the soul leaves the body. Although the work of the will differs greatly in childhood, in youth, in maturity, and in declining old age, the will always progresses, and the will is brought to perfection.[10]

Scivias (Know the Ways of the Lord) 1.4.21

⟋ This text is an excerpt from Hildegard's last, and most mature, visionary text, *Liber divinorum operum,* 1163–1173. This selection is from the beginning of the work, the first vision, where Hildegard writes of her vision of the origin of life.

[11] Hildegard begins this book by noting that God instructed her to write her visions down.

[12] The Holy Spirit is often depicted here as an image of a beautiful female form with a circlet of gold around her head.

[13] In Hildegard's work, the Holy Spirit is often depicted as the life-giving energy that is the root of all creation. This fiery divine energy joins with Wisdom and is found throughout the earth, and in the sun, the moon, and the stars.

☐ The Fiery Spirit

Again I heard a voice from heaven
instructing me, and it said:
Write what I tell you in this manner:[11]

And I saw amid the airs of the south
in the mystery of God
a beautiful, wondrous
image with a human form;
her face was so lovely and luminous
that it would be easier to look into the sun.
On her head she had
a broad circlet of gold.[12]

And the figure spoke:
I am the great and fiery energy,
I have kindled every living spark,[13]
and I have extinguished nothing mortal,
for I judge these things as they are.
I have determined the cosmos,
Flying around the circling circles
with my upper wings,
that is, with Wisdom.

I am the fiery life of divinity,
I blaze above the beautiful fields
I shine in the water,
I burn in the sun, the moon, and the stars.

LIBER DIVINORUM OPERUM (BOOK OF THE DIVINE WORKS) I.1

∼ Philip of Harvengt (d. ca. 1183) was a twelfth-century Premonstratensian, the abbot of Bonne-Espérance Abbey in Hainault (Belgium), and a theological writer. The Premonstratensian movement was founded by St. Norbert in 1120 and Premonstratensians lived lives of great austerity, common prayer, and celebrating the Eucharist. The abbey was founded in 1129. Norbert was a friend of Bernard of Clairvaux, and thus greatly influenced by the Cistercian movement. In this excerpt found at the beginning of the letter, Hildegard writes of the "blazing heart" that speaks to the inspiration of the Holy Spirit. Uncharacteristically, she includes some news of one of her own events in this letter. That is, that Philip went to hear her speak, probably during her last preaching journey, 1170–1173. Though very humbled by his presence, and adamant that her gifts were not her own, but God's, Hildegard once again compares herself to a feather carried by the wind.

14   A paraphrase of Hebrews 11:1: "Now faith is the substance of things hoped for, the evidence of things not seen."

15   Philip was a canon and his order "apostolic"; that is, they earned their own living, in contrast to orders that lived off endowments.

16   As Hildegard got older, her illnesses became chronic. An earlier letter from Philip suggests that the two might have been in regular contact.

☐ On the Faith of a Blazing Heart

The faith in God that one carries in a blazing heart through the inspiration of the Holy Spirit is truly glorious, when that person in true love embraces those things that cannot be seen, as if they were those things that can be seen and prized.[14] It is also a praiseworthy thing in you, that out of your love of God, you deigned to come and hear a weak and unlearned woman, like myself. A wind blew down from a high mountain and as it passed over ornamented castles and towers, it set in motion a small feather with no ability to fly on its own, but received its motion from the wind. Undoubtedly, God revealed this to show what a creature could accomplish through the Divine, when it could not presume to accomplish anything by itself.

However, you who stand in the office of the prophets, in whom the care of the apostolic order[15] has been bound, I ask that you please send your prayers to me, so that I may remain in God's grace. For you can see, I am still lying on my sickbed. I have no security in myself; I have placed all my hope and confidence in the mercy of God alone.[16]

TO ABBOT PHILIP OF HARVENGT, 1170–1173; *EPISTOLARIUM* (LETTERS) 180

Part 3
Divine Love

In Hildegard's texts, the mystery of divine love enfolds all in an interrelated universe; it is the matrix or womb in which humankind, along with the rest of creation, is born. In the context of Hildegard's visions, divine love speaks to the mystery found in the journey of life and death, and what it means to be made in the image of God. As Hildegard grew into greater understanding of her visions, she began to see divine love as the fecundity and primal life force at work in the universe. Hildegard uses rich symbols to describe divine love in her writing. For example, divine love is found in the power of redemption. Divine love also reveals itself as the ever-circling energy of the Trinity. Hildegard ultimately believed in a life-giving God for all, always beckoning us to divine love.

⬿ Adam of Ebrach (d. 1161) was the first abbot of Ebrach Abbey in Bamberg, Bavaria. In 1126 he led twelve monks from Morimond Abbey in Cologne to Franconia, to this new monastery, founded by King Conrad III and his wife, Gertrud. Adam was a highly powerful abbot and helped with other new foundations. He was a close friend of Bernard of Clairvaux and also had a major role in the Second Crusade. He was well known at the courts of the emperor and the pope. Several of his letters to and from Hildegard survive; he wrote on her behalf to the emperor, and also wrote to Hildegard directly seeking her spiritual and pastoral advice.

In this evocative text, Hildegard contemplates the experience of divine love. Like many of Hildegard's visions, this text is reminiscent of the book of Revelation.

1 In this vision, divine love is seen as a blindingly beautiful girl, bathed in light, brighter than a star, and holding the sun and the moon in her hands.

2 Hildegard clearly states her belief in God's love for all creatures. Though she believes that humankind is God's highest creation, all creatures, all species, share in divine love.

3 Like a loving parent, God foresaw the needs of all creatures and continues to love them throughout all eternity.

4 Although Hildegard certainly believed, like many of her contemporaries, in the reality of sin and the presence of evil in the world, it is noticeable that she balances these beliefs with a profound assertion that the most powerful force in the universe is love, and God lavishes that love on every creature.

The "matrix" she mentions here is another way to refer to the womb, or the womb that brings forth all life. Barbara Newman argues that here is an example of Hildegard's writing on *caritas*, or divine love, as the divine mother. For an extended explanation, see Barbara Newman, *Sister of Wisdom: St. Hildegard's Theology of the Feminine* (Berkeley: University of California Press, 1987), 63–64. Newman

☐ On God's Love for All Creatures

In a true vision of the spirit in a waking state:
I saw a likeness of the most beautiful girl[1]
with her face so aglow with a splendid brightness
that I could not really look upon her.
Her cloak was whiter than snow
and brighter than a star.
She held the sun and the moon in her right hand
and she embraced them tenderly.

And I heard a voice saying to me:
The girl whom you see is Divine Love,
who abides in eternity.
For when God wished to create the world
he bent down in tenderest love
and foresaw every need,
just like a father preparing an inheritance for his son.
In this way he carried out all his works
in a great burning fire of love.
Thus all creatures in every species[2]
and form acknowledge their creator,
because Love was the primal stuff
from which every creature was made.[3]
When God said: "Let it be done," it was done,
because Divine Love was the matrix from which every creature was made,
in the blink of an eye.[4]

To Abbot Adam of Ebrach, ca. 1166; *Epistolarium* (Letters) 85 R/A points out eloquently that the three archetypal mothers in Hildegard's visions—*caritas* (divine love), the Virgin Mary, and *ecclesia* (the church)—all brought Christ into the world through the flesh.

〜 In this text, Hildegard sees a vision of celestial love. We all love from the life power of God, which is eternal. Here celestial love is the first of three ascetical virtues, all in feminine form. (Discipline and modesty are the other two.)

5 Her hair is not covered, but loose and flowing; she wears no woman's head covering. The whiteness of her hair is symbolic of priestly celibacy, which Hildegard supports.

6 Note that the figure is a woman wearing both a bishop's miter and a pallium, an ecclesiastical garment bestowed by the pope. The color purple is also associated with the royal priesthood.

7 In Christian iconography, lilies symbolize eternal life and palms symbolize death or the promise of redemption made through God's love for humanity.

8 Not only does God love us as a lover does, but God loves us for all eternity.

☐ Celestial Love

The figure wore on her head a bishop's miter, and had loose white hair.[5] And she wore a white pallium, whose two borders were adorned on the inside with embroidered purple.[6] And in her right hand she held lilies and other flowers, and in her left had a palm.[7] She said: O sweet life, sweet embrace of eternal life, O blessed happiness in which there are eternal rewards. You are always so delightful that I am always satisfied with the inner joy that is in my God.[8]

SCIVIAS (KNOW THE WAYS OF THE LORD) 2.3.1

9   This particular psalm antiphon is cited by the Anonymous 4, a renowned women's a cappella medieval music group, in their release *The Origin of Fire* (2006) as perhaps the best known of Hildegard's compositions, with its long melismas and wide dramatic leaps when sung. The first phrase sums up Hildegard's belief in the inherent goodness, spiritually and materially, of all creation.

What is translated here as "love" or "lady love" is the Latin word *caritas*. A central theme in Hildegard's visions is the life force that animates every living thing.

"Here Caritas is in heaven what the Virgin Mary is on earth," notes Barbara Newman, "the queen consort of God—that divinely feminine spirit whom no effort or doctrine could ever quite exclude from his throne" (*Symphonia*, 279).

10   This text is a brief excerpt from a sermon Hildegard gave at her former monastery of Disibodenberg in 1171, preserved in the form of a letter to the abbot. The overall sermon focuses on Hildegard's explanation of the workings of God in all creation and through salvation history. Abbot Helengerus was the successor of Kuno, the abbot when Hildegard and her nuns left Disibodenberg. Correspondence indicates that Helengerus had his shortcomings, and Hildegard did not refrain from writing to him harshly on occasion, though he tried to make peace between the monasteries of Disibodenberg and Rupertsberg.

11   In this text, Hildegard refers to fire as the life-giving spirit that animates all of creation, as well as a symbol of the divine love of the Creator.

12   These last sentences refer to 1 John 4:18: "There is no fear in love; but perfect love casteth out fear: because fear hath torment. He that feareth is not made perfect in love."

☐ Love Flows Richly into All Things

Love flows richly into all things;
she is greatly exalted from the depths up to the stars
and most loving toward all things,
for she gave the highest king the kiss of peace.[9]

Symphonia (Songs) 25

☐ Divine Love Spreads like a Flame

The fire has a flame that the wind accelerates, so that the flame becomes a blazing fire.[10] Thus, the word is in the voice and the word is heard. The fire has a flame and it is praise to God, and the word is in the voice and it is praise to God; the wind moves the flame and it is praise to God, and the word is heard and it is praise to God. Thus all creation is praise to God.[11] The person who fears does not love; and they who do not praise cannot work. Divine love drives out fear and spreads like a flame.[12]

To Abbot Helengerus of Disibodenberg, ca. 1171; *Epistolarium* (Letters) 77R

~ This text is from a longer letter by Hildegard in response to five Cistercian abbots who wrote her in regard to the case of a noblewoman struggling with infertility. The woman herself brought the letter to Hildegard, and requested her prayers of assistance. Though compassionate, Hildegard is clear that while she will certainly pray for the woman and her husband, it is God alone who brings children. However, she uses the opportunity to send the abbots her reflections on humility. In this section, she writes of the voice of divine love and its place in the symphony of salvation.

13 In this text divine love has a resonant, echoing, ringing, sonorous voice—it reverberates through nature, it cries for the poor and the lame, and it resounds in heaven.

☐ The Voice of Divine Love

That same voice is a sounding trumpet in the embrace of divine love, for it resonates with kindness, and by means of humility gathers the meek, and with mercy anoints their wounds. The voice of divine love flows with the rushing water of the Holy Spirit and the peace of God's goodness. Humility plants a garden with every fruit tree of God's grace, encompassing all the greenness of God's gifts. Mercy soothes all the suffering of humankind with a balm. The voice of divine love resounds in the symphony of all praises of salvation. It resounds where it sees God, and where it fights against pride through humility. Through mercy it cries with a voice, at once both lamenting and joyful. It gathers unto itself the poor and the lame and seeks the help of the spirit in all things with good works. It resounds in the dwelling place of God, where the saints blaze in those places prepared for them while they were in the world.[13]

To Five Abbotts, 1157; Epistolarium (Letters) 70

Part 4
Holy Wisdom

Hildegard was well acquainted with wisdom literature as found in Scripture, and her visions of the divine feminine—Holy Wisdom, Sophia, Sapientia—relate to a variety of images and themes found throughout her texts, including the church, the Virgin Mary, Eve, and virginity. Hildegard believed that "Holy Wisdom" was the inspiration for all of Scripture. Though Hildegard often uses masculine images for God, she uses feminine images like Holy Wisdom to depict the divine embrace between God and all creation. She sees wisdom as the all-encompassing energy of God at work throughout the course of human history.

⟨∾⟩ This brief but evocative text is a hymn to Holy Wisdom, also known as Sophia. Hildegard frequently refers to Wisdom in her visions, usually in feminine form, but in this antiphon she appears in a more abstract form with three wings. This figure comes from several sources, as Barbara Newman suggests in *Symphonia*, 268. One is the image of Wisdom the creatrix from Sirach 24:8–9, who "circled the vault of heaven alone, and pierced into the depth of the abyss."

| 1 | In this stanza Holy Wisdom encircles and embraces all things in the journey of life. Newman states that when Hildegard writes of Wisdom as creatrix, using feminine rather than masculine imagery, she focuses on immanence as opposed to transcendence. Rather than the creator who calls the universe into being, the creatrix creates the cosmos by living within it, inferred here by the image of a circling motion. See *Sister of Wisdom*, 64–65.

| 2 | The three wings in this stanza may have multiple meanings, but it is likely that Hildegard intends to refer to the Trinity: the Father in heaven, the Son on earth, and the Spirit that fills all of creation.

| 3 | Newman observes that the verb for *sweat*, or *exudes moisture*, is used in reference to Jesus's sweating in the Garden of Gethsemane in Luke 22:44—"And being in an agony he prayed more earnestly: and his sweat was as it were great drops of blood falling down to the ground"—as well as the moisture exuded in nature that makes everything green and fruitful.

☐ O Power of Wisdom

O power of Wisdom![1]
who circling, circled,
embracing all things
in a single life-giving path.

You have three wings:[2]
one soars to the heavens,
the second exudes[3] moisture from the earth,
and the third soars everywhere.
All praise be to you, as is your due,
O Wisdom!

Symphonia (Songs) 2

~ *Ordo Virtutum* is a liturgical drama, or morality play, written and composed by Hildegard around 1151. It is the earliest morality play by more than a century, and the only surviving drama from the Middle Ages with a known author for both the text and the music. The play is about the struggle of a human soul, Anima, torn between the Virtues and the Devil. The happy soul is a reflection of God's wisdom and love. This excerpt includes the Prologue, in which the Virtues are introduced to the Patriarchs and Prophets, and the first section, where we hear the complaints of the souls imprisoned in bodies. Scholars believe that the play was written for the nuns of Hildegard's convent and performed for the dedication of the Rupertsberg church in 1152. There is only one male part in the play—the Devil—and a male chorus as the Prophets and Patriarchs. The play has parts for a woman's chorus and seventeen female virtues. The part of Anima, the soul, is also sung by a woman.

☐ Here Begins the Play of the Virtues

Prologue

Patriarchs and Prophets

Who are these, who seem like clouds?

Virtues

O Ancient holy ones of old,
why do you marvel at us?
The Word of God grows bright
in the form of man,
and thus we shine with him,
building the limbs of his beautiful body.

Patriarchs and Prophets

We are the roots, and you, the branches,
fruit of the living eye,
of which we are the shadow.

Scene 1

Lament of a Chorus of Embodied Souls

O, we are strangers here!
What have we done, straying to realms of sin?
We should have been daughters of the King,
but we have fallen into the shadow of sins.
O Living Sun, carry us on your shoulders
back to that most just heritage we lost in Adam!
O King of Kings, we are fighting in your battle.

(continued on page 51)

4   Anima is happy now, though she wants to skip life altogether and go straight to heaven. This is not allowed—she has to live first—and the Devil begins to tempt her with worldly ways.

5   This text is from a letter that Hildegard sent to Odo of Soissons (d. 1170), a frequent correspondent. He later went by the name of Odo of Paris once he became a master, or professor, at the university. It is from his correspondence that we know Hildegard's music was well known even when she was first starting to write down her visions. Odo heard about Hildegard at the Synod of Trier in 1147–1148. Although Odo had more theological training than Hildegard did, it is a sign of her spiritual authority that he writes her directly to ask theological questions.

Here Hildegard reports her message by way of the Living Light—the source of true Wisdom—rather than claiming authorship for herself. The "secret" word is divine revelation.

6   The letter focuses on the nature of divinity—that is, God is whole and cannot be divided. We know of God by God's work in the world—a trinity of activity, creativity, and perfection. Odo wrote to Hildegard in reaction to a scholastic controversy and looked to her for reassurance about the nature of the Trinity—specifically, that God is not one, but three unities.

Anima (joyfully)

O sweet divinity, O gentle life,
in which I wear a radiant robe,
accepting that which I lost in my first manifestation—
I cry for you and invoke all the Virtues.**4**

Virtues

You happy soul, sweet and divine creation,
fashioned in the great height of the wisdom of God,
you show great love.

Anima (joyfully)

Oh let me come to you joyfully,
that you may give me the kiss of your heart!

ORDO VIRTUTUM (PLAY OF THE VIRTUES)

☐ The Nature of God

The Living Light therefore speaks with the secret word of Wisdom:**5**
God is full and whole and beyond the beginning of time, and therefore
he cannot be divided or analyzed by words as a human being can. God
is a whole and nothing other than a whole, to which nothing can be
added and from which nothing can be taken away. For He-who-is is
both paternity and divinity, since it is said, "I am who I am." And He-
who-is is fullness itself. How is this to be understood? By his activity,
creativity, and perfection.**6**

TO ODO OF SOISSONS, 1148; EPISTOLARIUM (LETTERS) 39R

≈ Following ancient practice, Hildegard personified the virtues as beautiful young women. Wisdom is the first of the seven gifts of the Holy Spirit, and, in Hildegard's musical works, is always female.

7 In this text Wisdom is seen as co-creator, along with God and the Holy Spirit.

8 Throughout this text Hildegard contrasts the world of human beings with creation, as it is filled and embraced by God. Though evil is very real, it ultimately cannot destroy what is of God.

☐ Wisdom and Her Sisters

And I saw in the middle of that
southern region three forms,
two of them standing in the clearest fountain,
encircled and crowned above by a round, porous stone.
One was in shimmering purple,
and the other was in dazzling white.
The third stood outside that fountain
and beneath the stone,
dressed in glowing white.

And the first image said:
I am Love, the light of the living God,
and Wisdom carries out her tasks along with me.[7]
In the shadow, Wisdom
measures out all things equally,
so that one thing may not outbalance another,
and so that nothing may be moved by another
into its opposite.

For Wisdom rules and constrains
every sort of diabolical malice.[8]
In herself and through herself alone
she made all things lovingly and gently.
They can be destroyed by no enemy,
because she sees most truly
the beginning and the end of all things—
she who fully composed all things
so that all things might be ruled by her.

PROLOGUE, *LIBER DIVINORUM OPERUM* (BOOK OF THE DIVINE WORKS)

Part 5
Spiritual Community

While most of Hildegard's visionary texts show her mystical gifts and the scope of her religious imagination, in many ways her personality emerges the most through her letters. Many of Hildegard's letters are written to her extended "spiritual community" of both female and male spiritual leaders, and members of her own family, who came to her for advice, comfort, and understanding. A reformist visionary, Hildegard was dedicated to reviving the church from the inside, and was intolerant of clergy who used their office to increase their personal wealth or to enhance their position. Both firm and compassionate in her responses, she cared for the souls and spirits of many. Other religious of her day, some abbots and abbesses of prosperous abbeys, wrote to Hildegard when they grew weary of the trials of leadership or when they needed some practical advice. Hildegard was understanding of human frailties, but at the same time believed that abbots and abbesses, in particular, were given a sacred trust that was not to be abandoned lightly. Hildegard's letters show the extent of her influence beyond her home community, and the large numbers of people who believed they would benefit from her wisdom.

1 In this section from *Scivias*, Hildegard explains the orders of the church, using the metaphor of some basic foods. The vision strongly affirms Hildegard's faith in the hierarchy of the church.

2 Here Hildegard makes clear that monks outrank priests. People with religious vocations provide people with a simple diet and are adverse to worldly things.

3 Priests are useful to Hildegard, as long as they are providing pastorally for the people. They are like fruit, sweet, when they perform their duty.

4 Lastly, the laity are the meat, and fall into two categories—those who participate in the world of the flesh and have families, and those who live chastely and love virtue.

5 The text is from a letter to Odo of Paris (d. 1171), also known as Odo of Soissons, a theology master who later became a master, or professor, at the University of Paris, and became bishop of Tuscany in 1170. Though Hildegard always claimed she had no formal theological training, she had enough status and skill to discuss academic theology with him in an exchange of letters.

This brief excerpt is one version of Hildegard's famous saying, that she was no more than a "feather on the breath of God." In it she stresses that it is her complete trust in God, and not her own abilities, that sustains her visions. Odo's life was very much involved in the world of academic theology, and he honored Hildegard's abilities to the point that he would bring theological questions to her. While Hildegard was interested in theological reasoning, she drew the line when it interfered with the spiritual life. Here she is reminding Odo of that fact. (See Anne H. King-Lenzmeier, *Hildegard of Bingen: An Integrated Vision* [Collegeville, MN: Liturgical Press, 2001], 81–83.)

☐ Monks, Clergy, and Laity

Those who are avowed monks are the grain that provides the people
with simple and wholesome food.[1] In this way, God's people are bitter and harsh to the taste of worldly things.[2] The priests are the fruit,
sweet-tasting; thus, priests are sweet to people in performing their useful office.[3] The common laity are regarded as meat, among which there
is also clean poultry, for by their existence in the world of the flesh they
have children. Among them are also followers of chastity, such as wid-
ows and ascetics, who soar to heavenly heights through their appetite
for good virtues.[4]

SCIVIAS (KNOW THE WAYS OF THE LORD) 2.5, 37

☐ A Feather on the Breath of God

Listen: A king sat upon his throne, surrounded by lofty and wonderfully
beautiful columns, ornamented with ivory and bearing the banners of
the king proudly to all. Then it pleased the king to lift a small feather
from the ground, and he commanded it to fly. Yet a feather does not fly
because of anything in itself, but because the air bears it along. Thus,
I am a feather on the breath of God, not gifted with great powers or
education, nor even with good health, but I rely completely on God.[5]

TO ODO OF PARIS, CA. 1148–1149; EPISTOLARIUM (LETTERS) 40R

〰 This deeply sad letter was written to Richardis after Hildegard realized that she could do nothing to prevent the young woman's departure from Rupertsberg to become an abbess in a distant diocese. Not only was Richardis Hildegard's assistant in writing the *Scivias* (along with Volmar), but she was also one of the closest confidantes of her life. When she learned that Richardis's family arranged for the appointment, she was desolate. This letter shows the many emotions surging through Hildegard, as she desires to do the will of God, but at the same time is reluctant to give up a human relationship that is very important to her. Throughout the letter the reader can sense the tension within Hildegard between doing the right thing in terms of her monastic vocation and learning not to put her trust in things of the world, and coming to terms with her deep sadness at the thought of a separation from Richardis. The two women never had the opportunity to resolve the events of their separation in person; Richardis died before she could return to Rupertsberg, and Hildegard never saw her dear spiritual daughter alive again.

6 | In the opening of the letter, Hildegard reminds herself (and perhaps Richardis) that she erred in putting her love for a particular person above her love for God, though it is unclear by what follows if she really has resolved her feelings.

7 | Here feelings rise up in Hildegard again, and she uses a quotation taken from Jesus's Passion, when he asks God from the cross why he has been abandoned, "My God, my God, why hast thou forsaken me?" See Psalm 21:2, Matthew 27:46, and Mark 15:34.

8 | Hildegard admits that she so loved Richardis that many others asked questions about the appropriateness of singling her out from others in the community. In referring to herself as an orphan, she is recalling the passage in John 14:18, where Jesus promises the disciples he will not leave them comfortless, but will always be with them.

9 | Hildegard expresses her grief, but, as a mother would, wishes Richardis safety and happiness.

☐ Separation from Richardis Brings Deep Sorrow

Hear me, daughter. Your mother is talking to you in the spirit: My sorrow rises up, my grief is destroying the great faith and consolation I had in human beings. From now on let me say: "It is better to trust in the Lord, than to put confidence in princes." As this Scripture says, a person should look to the living height, with vision unobstructed by earthly love and the lessening of faith, which the airy humor of the earth renders transitory. A person thus looking to God fixes his sight to the sun like an eagle. And for this reason one should not pay attention to a person of high birth, for such a person withers as the flower fails. I erred thus because of my love of a noble person.[6]

Now I say to you: As many times as I sinned in this way, God showed that sin to me either through some difficulties, or through some sorrows, just as he now has done regarding you, as you well know.

Now, again I say: Woe is me, mother, woe is me, daughter. "Why have you forsaken me"[7] like an orphan? I loved the nobility of your character, your wisdom, your chastity, your soul, and your entire life, so that many people said to me: What are you doing?[8]

Now let all those who have a sorrow like mine, mourn with me, all who in the love of God, have had such great love in their hearts and minds for a person—as I had for you—but who was seized in a moment from them—just as you were taken from me. But may the angel of God go before you, and may his mother keep you safe. Remember your sorrowing mother Hildegard, so that your happiness may not fail.[9]

To Abbess Richardis of Stade, ca. 1151–1152, *Epistolarium* (Letters) 64

⟨∿⟩ Hartwig was the brother of Richardis of Stade, the close confidante and protégée of Hildegard. (Both were cousins of Hildegard's mentor, Jutta of Sponheim.) As the bishop of the diocese where Richardis was appointed abbess, in Bassum, he was the authority who could order her to return to Rupertsberg. This letter was written after Richardis's death, when both parties were still in deep mourning. Hildegard is responding to a letter in which Hartwig assures her that Richardis died after receiving the sacraments of the church, and with tearful longing for Hildegard and her former convent. According to her brother, Richardis was prepared to return to Rupertsberg as soon as she could obtain permission to do so, but death intervened. Despite all the pain and struggle that Richardis's departure caused her, Hildegard responds to Richardis's brother with kindness and love.

10 Richardis was called "daughter" when she lived as a nun under Hildegard's authority, but was also viewed as Hildegard's "mother" when she became abbess in a more prestigious abbey than Hildegard's. Hildegard explains the basis for her love of Richardis: they were brought together by divine love, and a vision from the Living Light.

11 In this passage Hildegard once again stresses her belief in the status and sanctity of virginity as the most sacred state of life possible. The phrase "daughters of Zion rejoice" is taken from Zachariah: "Rejoice greatly, O daughter of Zion; shout, O daughter of Jerusalem: behold, thy King cometh unto thee: he is just, and having salvation" (9:9).

12 In this section, Hildegard explains the way she viewed Richardis: as a beautiful and wise noblewoman. And while Richardis was admired and had a worldly position, in the end it was her heavenly bridegroom, Jesus, who made sure that she ultimately was with him forever.

13 At the end of the letter, Hildegard admits that she was deeply hurt by his refusal to return Richardis to Rupertsberg, but she doesn't hold it against him, and she hopes that Hartwig performs the good works his sister wished.

☐ Solace for Richardis's Brother after Her Death

O how great is the salvation of those souls, looked upon by God with no hint of his shadow in them. He works in them like a mighty warrior, defeated by no one, so that his victory may be sure.

Just so, dear one, was the case of my daughter Richardis, whom I call both my daughter and my mother, for my soul was full of divine love for her, as the Living Light taught me to do in a most powerful vision.[10]

God held her in such high regard that the pleasures of the world could not embrace her. She always fought against it, even though she appeared like a flower in beauty and grace in the harmony of this world. When she was yet among us, I heard the following said about her in a true vision: "O virginity, you stand in the royal bridal chamber." Now in the virginal branch, she has been made part of that most sacred order, and the daughters of Zion rejoice.[11] But the ancient serpent wished to deprive her of that sacred honor, using the nobility of her worldly position. But the mighty Judge drew this, my daughter, to himself, cutting her off from all human glory. Therefore, although the world loved her beautiful appearance and her worldly wisdom while she was still alive, my soul has great confidence in her salvation. But God loved her more, and so did not wish to give his love to a rival lover, that is, the world.[12]

Now, dear Hartwig, sitting as Christ's representative, fulfill the desire of your sister's soul, as obedience demands. And as she always had your interests at heart, so now you must champion her soul, and do good deeds according to her desires. Now I, too, shall cast that sadness from my heart, which you have caused me on account of my daughter. May God grant you, through the prayers of the saints, the dew of his grace and a blessed reward in the life to come.[13]

To Hartwig of Stade, Archbishop of Bremen, 1152; *Epistolarium* (Letters) 18

⟨∾⟩ It is not clear if this letter was sent to Abbot Kuno (d. 1155) or his successor, Abbot Helengerus. However, in this excerpt Hildegard justifies her reasons for moving her community to St. Rupertsberg just a few years earlier. That episode was definitely a key event in her relationship with Kuno, more than with his successor, because he was the superior who attempted to deny her permission to begin the new foundation. Kuno ended up losing all control of the nuns, including control over the wealth from their families and the stature they brought to Disibodenberg. This letter was sent during a time of heated negotiations about financial matters. The issues of control and finances were not completely resolved during Hildegard's lifetime. In this letter Hildegard explains that she visited the monastery at Disibodenberg, and the visit did not go well.

14 Apparently, Hildegard visited Disibodenberg and some, though not all, of the monks threatened her in the hope that she would leave. It seems the events leading to her departure from the monastery, and the setting up of her new foundation, were not universally appreciated by the monks. This letter suggests that more of the monks than Abbot Kuno objected to Hildegard's move to Rupertsberg. Beyond the loss of fame and income the monastery experienced when Hildegard established her own foundation, some of the monks may have also felt betrayed on a personal level. After all, Hildegard was raised in their midst from the time she was eight years old, so it is not unreasonable to assume that some of the monks felt angry for personal reasons. Also, given the patriarchal culture of church and society, the monks' anger at a woman who repeatedly insisted on her independence from their governance was not unusual, which is perhaps why she felt a need to make clear that her departure was the will of God, and for her to stay at Disibodenberg would have shortened her life.

15 From Psalm 22:7–8: "All they that see me laugh me to scorn: they shoot out the lip, they shake the head, saying, He trusted on the Lord that he would deliver him: let him deliver him, seeing he delighted in him."

16 Here Hildegard refers to the monastery at Disibodenberg as her "mother," or the place that gave birth to her religious vocation.

☐ Hildegard Justifies Moving Her Community to Rupertsberg

You who are my father in your office—and I am happy to say it—I pray that now you may be to me a father in deed. I paid a visit to the place where God had entrusted you with the staff of his authority. But an angry mob of some of your monks rose up and gnashed their teeth at me, as if I were a bird of gloom or a terrible beast, and they bent their bows against me in order to scare me away. I know for a fact that God rescued me from that place for his own inexplicable reasons; I believe I would have died before my time if I had stayed there, for my soul was so disturbed by God's revelations.[14]

Blessing and salvation upon those who received me with affection; may God have mercy, according to his will, on those who were shaking their heads at me.[15] Alas, my mother,[16] with what sadness and disappointment you received me.

TO THE ABBOT OF DISIBODENBERG, CA. 1155; *EPISTOLARIUM* (LETTERS) 75

 In a letter to Hildegard, the abbess of the Convent of St. Theodore and St. Maria in Bamberg expresses a deep affection and a devout respect for her. Hildegard's response contains a sizable number of letters from other nuns, and specifically other abbesses, which suggests an expansive network of support and friendship across the miles. In her letter to Hildegard, the abbess asks Hildegard for encouragement, for she is weary, and asks to be relieved of her responsibilities and join Hildegard's community.

17 In the first two paragraphs of the letter, Hildegard encourages her sister abbess to remain where she is, as it is why God created her. Though she may at the time be "obscured by black clouds," perhaps depression, Hildegard encourages the abbess to look beyond this to the reasons why God chose her for this position. Hildegard also reminds the abbess that she will be held accountable for doing the work her master intended.

18 Here Hildegard tries to help her friend see her gifts for the position. The frequent complaint of those in religious leadership, then and now, is that they have no leisure time. Hildegard acknowledges that reality, and, perhaps not surprisingly for someone with her prodigious accomplishments, is less than sympathetic. Instead, she reminds her friend that bad things happen when people have too much free time, anyway. She recommends that her friend focus on the firmament as a means of pulling herself out of her depression.

19 Lastly, Hildegard suggests that the abbess demand obedience from her daughters. She acknowledges the isolation of the leader, or the one who is feared. It is important to remember that while some people adored Hildegard, some members of her community did complain about her high standards. She demands a high standard of herself, and those in her community, and advises the Abbess of Bamberg to do the same, for therein lies her eternal reward.

☐ The Need for Discipline

Mother, a man who has a field and does not till it and make it fruitful is neglectful, because he does not work for the reward from the heart of his master. Think who made the ox and the ass. God created them to serve humankind. So why should not a person work to fulfill his proper, useful function, since he is wholly the handiwork of God and God would not make him to be vain and useless?

For God made humanity like the firmament that bears the sun, the moon, and the stars to give light to the whole of creation, and mark the times and the seasons. But if they were all obscured by black clouds, then creation would fear that its end is near.[17]

Daughter of God, know that you are this field, because you embrace the people with your goodwill, and thus they can accept your words and deeds. So don't avoid working with the people, and don't abandon them for lack of leisure time, for frequently useless weeds will grow wherever there is idleness. Put before yourself a vision of the firmament, so that you do not hide the light of your reason behind black clouds of evil, as if you were barely alive.[18]

Therefore, you should restrain and discipline your daughters in all matters. Just as a child fears being beaten with a rod, so must the one in authority be feared by everyone. Do not be afraid to punish them in this way, for in doing so you will increase your reward in the life everlasting, so that the breath of the Holy Spirit may flow in you.[19]

TO THE ABBESS OF BAMBERG, CA. 1158–1161; *EPISTOLARIUM* (LETTERS) 61R

~ Gertrude of Stahleck (ca. 1104–1191) was a countess, the sister of King Conrad III, and the aunt of the emperor when she was widowed and decided to enter the religious life. In this letter Hildegard rejoices at Gertrude's religious vocation, believing it is a high calling. The letter is rich with scriptural images.

20 The passage beginning "the voice of the turtledove ..." is from the Song of Songs and signifies a time of rejoicing: "For, lo, the winter is past, the rain is over and gone; the flowers appear on the earth; the time of the singing of birds is come, and the voice of the turtle[dove] is heard in our land" (Song of Songs 2:11–12).

21 The reference to the lone turtledove here is to Gertrude's widowhood.

22 This image is also from the Songs of Songs: "As the lily among thorns, so is my love among the daughters" (2:2).

23 Here Hildegard writes that, despite Gertrude's wealth, when she chose the spiritual life, she shone when she entered the convent. The rose of Jericho is also known as the "resurrection flower." The phrase "the Son of God called thorns" is a reference to the parable of the sower, where Jesus explains that the word of God is like seed scattered in our hearts. The seed will bear fruit in accordance with the condition of our hearts. "That which fell among thorns are they, which, when they have heard, go forth, and are choked with cares and riches and pleasures of this life, and bring no fruit to perfection" (Luke 8:14).

☐ Giving Up the World for God

Daughter of God, in the pure knowledge of faith, hear these words spoken to you: "The voice of the turtledove is to be heard in our land."[20] This is the Son of God, who, contrary to the laws of the flesh, was born from the untilled earth, the flesh of the Virgin Mary. And the flowers of all the virtues came forth, sweet with the fragrances of the virtues. For the garden of these virtues arose in the prodigal son, who, when he came to his senses, ran to confess his sins to his father, that is, to the omnipotent Father. And his Father received him with the kiss of the humanity of his Son.

When with our own will we give up the world for the love of God, then the voice of the turtledove is heard, for above all other birds the turtledove remains alone when she loses her mate.[21] Dearest daughter, you also did this when you gave up the pomp of this world. How beautiful were your shoes, daughter of the king, when for the love of God, you entered upon the straight and narrow path of the spiritual life! Therefore rejoice, daughter of Zion, for the Holy Spirit dwells in the center of your heart. Consider that your Comforter created you "as a lily among the thorns,"[22] when you chose the spiritual life, although you still had the pomp and riches of this world, which the Son of God called thorns. And in your passion for your entry into the order, you shone red like a rose of Jericho.[23]

I have to rejoice in you, because what I have heard and desired for you is now complete; so you should rejoice with me, too. I hope with true faith that you become a wall adorned with precious stone and pearls in the sight of God, and that you will be praised by the heavenly host. Rejoice and be glad in God, for you will live forever.

To Gertrude of Stahleck, after 1161; *Epistolarium* (Letters) 62R

～ Although Hildegard entered the religious life at the age of eight, she remained in touch with her family members. This brief letter to her brother Hugo is one such example, and proof that even saints come from very human families!

Many of Hildegard's siblings went into the church as well. Her brother Hugo, who was her secretary for a brief time after Volmar's death, was the precentor (the person in charge of worship and the choir) at Mainz Cathedral. Roricus, who is mentioned in the letter, was a canon at the cathedral in Thorley in the Saar region. The exact source of the conflict between the two men is unknown. Whatever it was, Hildegard felt compelled to intervene.

24 Hildegard is willing to admit to Hugo that sometimes exaggerated rumors are circulated throughout the world of the church. Because of this reality, she advises Hugo not to accuse his brother Roricus unjustly, or to speak badly of him.

25 Hildegard cautions her brother about his poor anger management, lest he anger God.

☐ A Family Conflict

The church frequently reports extraordinary things, and sometimes they are exaggerated beyond the truth and become ludicrous. Therefore, I advise you not to accuse your brother Roricus unjustly in your heart, and not to move beyond the bounds in speaking depraved words about him. God knows that you do not act rightly in this matter.[24]

Beware that your Lord does not blame you for this anger of yours and other similar matters.[25] May God pardon you for all your sins.

To Her Brother Hugo, ca. 1170; *Epistolarium* (Letters) 208

~ In this excerpt Hildegard requests support for her community from Pope Alexander III (ca. 1100–1181), born Roland of Siena, who spent much of his papacy fighting Emperor Frederick Barbarossa and his three antipopes. Hildegard wrote this letter near the end of her life, and it is an example of her continued conflicts with the monastery of Disibodenberg concerning the independence of her religious community since 1147. This text is an excerpt of a letter Hildegard wrote to the pope, explaining that after the death of her beloved Volmar in 1173, Abbot Helengerus of Disibodenberg refused to allow the nuns of St. Rupertsberg to elect their own provost to succeed him. This right, contends Hildegard, was granted them in their charter from the Archbishop of Mainz in 1158, and confirmed by Emperor Frederick Barbarossa in 1163. As a result of the conflict, Rupertsberg was without a provost for over a year. The nuns, and Hildegard in particular, were not interested in a priest they did not choose themselves. Hildegard worked assiduously to bring the conflict to an end, and outlasted her opposition. The pope sent Wezlinus, abbot of St. Andrew's Abbey in Cologne and Hildegard's nephew, as his emissary. He successfully negotiated with the abbot to assign the monk Gottfried as provost and secretary to Hildegard. Gottfried used the opportunity to begin Hildegard's biography, though he died before he could complete the project.

26 Here Hildegard is careful to address the pope in humility before she lays out the problem as she sees it. Though she claims that they need a priest to look after her community, she is also clear that they expect to have some say in the decision.

27 This quotation is taken from the parable of the talents in Matthew 25:14–30. The moral of this story is that we each must take care of what God has entrusted to us, no matter how much or how little. Hildegard reminds the pope that those who do the will of God are rewarded in heaven.

28 This is related to the Benedictine phrase "listen with the ears of your heart."

☐ Conflicts with the Monks at Disibodenberg

Now, O gentle Father, my sisters and I bend our knees before your paternal piety, praying that you deign to look upon the need of this poor little woman. We are now in great distress, because the abbot of Disibodenberg and his brothers deny us our privilege of election. We always had this privilege and we always took great care to retain it. If they will not grant us God-fearing and religious monks, such as we see, all feeling for religion will be destroyed among us. Therefore, my lord, help us for God's sake, so that we can have the man we elected, or freely ask to seek out and receive others, wherever we can, who will look after us and our interests, according to the will of God.[26]

Now again, we ask you, most pious Father, not to despise our petition or our messengers, who on the advice of our faithful friend, took on our cause. May you grant that which they seek to obtain from you, so that at the end of this life, which already hastens toward evening, you may reach the never-failing light and hear the sweet voice of the Lord, saying: "Well done, good and faithful servant. Because thou hast been faithful over a few things, I will place thee over many things: enter thou into the joy of the Lord."[27] Therefore, incline the ears of your piety[28] to our prayers, and be the bright day to us and to them, so that from the kindness of your generosity we may rejoice together in the Lord, and you may ever rejoice in eternal felicity.

TO POPE ALEXANDER III, CA.1173; *EPISTOLARIUM* (LETTERS) 59

⟨∿⟩ This powerful letter was written in response to a letter from Volmar, Hildegard's closest friend, scribe, and confessor. In his letter, Volmar wrote of his concern about the community after Hildegard's death. Obviously, they would be deprived of her person and her spiritual authority, as all the church will be. (Actually, Volmar predeceases Hildegard by six years.) But Volmar's concerns are also certainly logical. Hildegard's letter in response goes in a related, but different direction. Hildegard argues that from the time of the late 1140s it was God's will that the Rupertsberg convent separate from the monastery, and even after that separation occurred and received the approval of the emperor in 1163, she was embattled with the abbot and the monks about matters of income and property until her death in 1179. By the time of this letter, Hildegard had been dealing with them for more than twenty years and was realistically concerned that her nuns would lose their independence after her death, or at least that attempts would be made to curtail them.

29 The phrase "offer to God a sacrifice of praise" comes from Hebrews 13:15, where we are taught to bring God praises, in contrast to the old system of burnt offerings and animal sacrifices: "Let us offer the sacrifice of praise to God continually, that is, the fruit of our lips giving thanks to his name."

30 Hildegard asserts that her daughters have lived holy lives in the monastery that she founded, with the permission of her superiors. The paragraph establishes her line of reasoning for the letter.

31 Hildegard reiterates in the letter that she not only moved from Disibodenberg, but also that it was understood that the financial arrangements made for all the nuns went with them. She reminds them that these arrangements were made in accordance with the Rule of St. Benedict.

32 In Genesis 32:22–32, Jacob wrestled with an angel and could not overpower him. Jacob demanded that the angel give him a blessing before leaving, and the angel blessed him by changing his name to Israel, meaning "he wrestles with God."

☐ Advice to Her Nuns in the Event of Her Death

O daughters, you have followed in the footsteps of Christ in loving chastity, have chosen me as your mother, poor little woman that I am, a choice made in humble obedience to exalt God, not from myself, but from the Divine. I say to you with my maternal heart: This monastery I founded is the resting place of the relics of blessed Rupert the Confessor, to whose protection you have fled, manifest in miracles through the will of God, offering in a sacrifice of praise.[29] I came to this place with permission of my superiors and freely made it home for myself and all who should come after me.[30]

But later, through the advice of God, I went to visit Mount St. Disibod, from which I had seceded with permission, and presented my proposal before all who dwelt there: I asked that our monastery, and all the proceeds of the donations thereto, be not tied but set free from them, for the salvation of our souls, and the strict observance of the Rule.* And all conceded this freedom to me, and guaranteed it in writing. All those who saw, from the highest to the lowest, heard, and understood it, had great goodwill toward these matters, since they had been confirmed in writing by the will of God.[31] Let all who adhere to God learn and affirm this matter in goodwill, and perfect it and defend it, so that they may receive the same blessing that God gave to Jacob and Israel."[32]

But O, what great sorrow you will have, my daughters, after the death of your mother, for you will no more be able to suckle her breasts. For a long time with groans and sorrow you will tearfully say: "Alas, alas! We would eagerly suckle our mother's breasts, if she were with us now!" Therefore, O daughters of God, I admonish you to love one another, just as I, your mother, have advised you since my childhood, as you may be the brightest light among the angels, and vigorous in your spirits, just as your father Benedict taught you. May the Holy Spirit

(continued on page 75)

33 In this section, Hildegard assures her nuns that, while they will grieve after her death, they should refrain from discord, and live in love according to the Rule of St. Benedict. As the nun's superior since 1136, over thirty years, Hildegard may have been aware of how much she was responsible for the discipline and the management of the monastery, and thus, she had concerns about how the nuns would carry on without her.

34 Here she asserts her belief that the nuns will be valiant and upright after her death, but should any of them want to cause further discord, she prays that the Holy Spirit will root it out of them.

35 This closing sentence is a charge reminding the nuns that their monastery was hard won, and they should continue to live in it with intention, thus earning their place in heaven.

36 This appendix is an angry addition to the letter, warning of the repercussions should the abbot and monks of Disibodenberg decide to renege on the contract they made with Rupertsberg, and attempt to take away some of the property or their support, in addition to making regular verbal assaults. Given that the nuns of Rupertsberg were noblewomen, each came to the convent with an endowment, or "dowry," which went with her into the religious life. These dowries could be in the form of currency or land. This wealth was lost to Disibodenberg when the nuns left with Hildegard. Through painstaking negotiation, and calling in powerful people, Hildegard secured the wealth for Rupertsberg, but had to continue to protect it for the rest of her life.

grant you his gifts, because after my death you will no longer hear my voice. Never forget the sound of my voice among you, for it so often resounded in love.[33]

The hearts of my daughters now are grieved in their hearts for the sadness they feel for their mother, and they sigh and look heavenward. Later, they will shine with a bright and radiant light through the grace of God, and they will become valiant soldiers in the house of God. Therefore, if any one of my daughters wishes to cause discord and division in the spiritual discipline of this house, may the gift of the Holy Spirit root it out from her heart. Yet, if she should do this out of scorn for God, may the hand of the Lord strike it down before all people, for such a one should be confounded.[34]

Therefore, O daughters, live in this place in which you have chosen to fight for God, with all devotion and steadfastness, so you will earn your heavenly reward in it.[35]

At this point in the letter, some manuscripts add the following appendix:[36]

According to my true vision, I said this to the father abbot of the monastery: "The Serene Light says you should be a father to this community planted in my visions, for the salvation of the souls of my daughters. The donations settled upon them have nothing to do with you or your brothers, but your monastery should be a place of sanctuary for them.

(continued on page 77)

37 The reference to the Amalekites is from 1 Samuel 30:1–3: "And it came to pass, when David and his men were come to Ziklag on the third day, that the Amalekites had invaded the south, and Ziklag, and smitten Ziklag, and burned it with fire; and had taken the women captives, that were therein: they slew not any, either great or small, but carried them away, and went on their way. So David and his men came to the city, and, behold, it was burned with fire; and their wives, and their sons, and their daughters, were taken captives." Antiochus was a Greek king who sacked Jerusalem and executed many Jews. See 1 Maccabees 1:23f; 6:12.

38 Hildegard uses one of God's most revered names, revealed to Moses in Exodus 3:14: "And God said unto Moses, I am that I am: and he said, Thus shalt thou say unto the children of Israel, 'I am' hath sent me unto you.'"

39 The phrase "sons of Belial" is taken from 1 Samuel 2:12: "Now the sons of Eli were sons of Belial; they knew not the Lord." This is also translated: "Eli's sons were scoundrels; they had no regard for the Lord" (NIV).

But if your will is to continue gnashing your teeth with verbal assaults, then you are like the Amalekites and like Antiochus, who, as it is written, stripped bare the temple of the Lord.[37] If any among you say with scorn, "We intend to diminish their holdings," then "I Who Am" says you are the worst sort of despoilers.[38] If you attempt to take from us the shepherd of spiritual medicine, then again I say to you that you are like the sons of Belial,[39] and that in this matter you are not bearing in mind the justice of God, and then, the justice of God will destroy. And then with these words, I, a poor form of a woman, sought from the abbot and his brothers the freedom of our monastery and the unencumbered possession of my daughters' dowries....

TO THE NUNS AT RUPERTSBERG, CA. 1170; *EPISTOLARIUM* (LETTERS) 195

Part 6
Noble Greenness

One of the most original terms used by Hildegard in her texts is *viriditas*, or "greenness," meaning the vital life force that animates creation, also known as the "greening power of God." Hildegard describes this greenness as the eternal power that gives life to everything. This same life-giving greenness continues to infuse the world with life throughout the course of salvation history; it enables us to have a relationship with God that is growing and sustaining, both physically and spiritually. For Hildegard, to be green was to be more receptive to the Divine Presence in humanity and in creation. Greenness is also associated with moisture, and the nurture and fertility of all growth. The soul, in Hildegard's language, is called the "moisture drawn from the earth" or the "green life source of the flesh." Hildegard sometimes speaks of the Holy Spirit as "green fire" because it is the fire of God that animates all life. Jesus is seen as the "green word," referring to his life-giving action on the cross. Greenness produces fruit, and blossoms, and beauty in the world, and every creature possesses some of this divine illumination. Some scholars suggest that the inspiration for Hildegard's affection for all that is green was the lush beauty around the countryside of her home, which both inspired her and nurtured her soul.

〰️ For Hildegard, *viriditas*, or "greenness," refers to the vital force or life-giving energy that is at work in all of creation. God breathed *viriditas* into Adam and Eve. Adam was formed by the greenness of God's finger, or the Holy Spirit, who fills the world with sumptuous beauty and life. In Hildegard's worldview, *viriditas* is also the Spirit of God at work in us, bringing spiritual life and transformation, through the church in the world, and through all of creation. Greening or greenness is also associated with human creativity and the idea of humanity fully alive and in harmony with God and creation. In this responsory, written for her religious community to commemorate the Irish saint Disibod (ca. 619–700), Hildegard stresses the green-fingeredness of God. The image resonates with the idea of God at work in creation and the vitality of the Holy Spirit working within her monastic community. Beverly Mayne Kienzle points out that the Holy Spirit "animates the power of the greenness of the universe, touching and kissing the sinful soul in need of healing" (see *Homilies on the Gospels*, 8).

1 The image of the vineyard is common in medieval literature to describe the image of the church in the world, or a particular religious community.

2 Mountains are traditionally sites of religious encounter. Benedictine monasteries, such as Disibodenberg, were often built on top of mountains.

3 Disibod was an exile in that he never returned to Ireland after journeying to the continent in 653. Yet his ministry was "green" in that he obtained many followers and built his community on the eastern slopes of a mountain near Bingen.

4 Hildegard believed that all of life was preparation for the final journey of the soul for God. In this way, Disibod is a glorious example of a saintly life.

☐ Greenness of God's Finger

Greenness of God's finger,
through you God has planted a vineyard[1]
that gleams on high
like a carved pillar.

Response

You are glorious in God's preparation.

O height of the mountain[2]
You shall never be brought low
in God's judgment.
Yet you stand in the distance
like an exile.[3]
But there is no armed power
to seize you.

Response

You are glorious as God's preparation.[4]

Symphonia (Songs) 42

⟨∼⟩ This song to the Virgin Mary is considered one of Hildegard's masterpieces. In it she develops the theme of greenness in relation to the Virgin Mary as both the greenest branch and a beautiful flower.

5 Barbara Newman suggests that this image comes from the idea of Mary's fertility, from which she is assimilated into many of the trees of life in Scripture, such as the root of Jesse (Isaiah 11:1), the tree of Wisdom (Sirach 24), and the tree "planted in streams of water," in Psalm 1. Because of her virginity, however, she is most like the dry yet blooming branch of Aaron (Numbers 17:1–11). (See *Sister of Wisdom*, 192–193.) In this context, her arid *viriditas*, or greenness, stands for fertility without sexuality.

6 In Hildegard's poetry, *pigmentarius* (spice merchant or herbalist) also means "priest." Mary is not only the source for the Eucharistic body, but she is also the paradigm of a priest, as she made the incarnation possible (see Newman, *Sister of Wisdom*, 194).

7 See Isaiah 45:8: "Drop down, ye heavens, from above, and let the skies pour down righteousness: let the earth open, and let them bring forth salvation, and let righteousness spring up together; I the LORD have created it."

8 The most life-giving part of Mary is her womb; the wheat refers to the Eucharist. Hildegard writes that only wheat is used for the Eucharist because it is a dry and pure grain, free of pith, as Mary was free from "the pith of man." (See Newman, *Symphonia*, 277.)

9 See Matthew 13:31–32: "Another parable put he forth unto them, saying, The kingdom of heaven is like to a grain of mustard seed, which a man took, and sowed in his field: which indeed is the least of all seeds: but when it is grown, it is the greatest among herbs, and becometh a tree, so that the birds of the air come and lodge in the branches thereof."

☐ Hail O Greenest Branch

Hail O greenest branch![5]
You came forth in the blowing wind
of the quest of the saints.

When the time came
for you to blossom in your branches,
hail, hail to you,
for the heat of the sun exuded from you
an aroma like balsam.

For the beautiful flower sprang from you
that gave fragrance
to all the spices[6] that had dried out.

And they all appeared
in their strength and greenness.

So the skies rained dew upon the grass[7]
and all the earth was made glad;
because her womb brought forth wheat,[8]
and the birds of the heavens built their nests in it.[9]
Then a harvest was made ready for humans,
which brings great rejoicing for the banqueters.
in you, O sweet Virgin,
in you no joy is lacking.

Eve rejected all these things.
Now let us praise the most high.

Symphonia (Songs) 19

10   In this responsory song about virginity, Hildegard refers to greenness as the vital force that is found in all creation. Greening or greenness is also associated with human creativity and the idea of humanity fully alive and in harmony with God and creation. In this form, responsorial verses are repeated between the verses of the song.

For Hildegard, virginity is the highest state of human life, and comparable to the beauty found in creation—in the sun, in the red dawn, in divinity, and the like. The beauty of the virgin will never fade, but will always remain green.

11   Throughout her religious life, Hildegard consistently advised against excessive abstinence and bodily mortification in favor of moderate asceticism. In the introductory paragraph, Hildegard explains her response to visions from the Living Light and how excessive abstinence hurts the body and leads to vanity and arrogance. Here "greenness" is related to the life-giving power of food to provide nourishment and fuel for the body; excessive abstinence leads to unvirtuous behavior. The virtues have "greenness," but humility and love die in situations where excessive abstinence prevails.

☐ O Noblest Greenness

O noblest greenness,
you have roots in the sun,
and you shine in dazzling serenity,
in a sphere
that no earthly excellence comprehends.[10]

Response

You are enclosed
in the embrace of divine mysteries.

You glow like the red dawn,
and burn like a flame of the sun.

Response

You are enclosed
in the embrace of divine ministries.

SYMPHONIA (SONGS) 56

☐ Excessive Abstinence Withers Greenness

The Living Light says: Dry sand is useless and earth that is overplowed will not yield good fruit. Dry, rocky ground produces only thorns and useless weeds. In much the same way, excessive and immoderate abstinence does harm to the body, for it withers away without receiving the greenness of proper nourishment. Where a lack of moderation prevails, the ethereal virtues, that is, humility and the beautiful flowers of love, die because excessive abstinence lacks the greenness of the virtues.[11]

(continued on page 87)

12   In this section Hildegard explains that just as it is not advisable to deprive oneself of food and drink, it is also inappropriate for those who claim to be religious to eat and drink rich foods, which lead to lust. Instead, those who wish to live a chaste life need to eat and drink in moderation.

13   This last section appears to be a quote from Christ in one of Hildegard's visions. He emphasizes that immoderate practices are not necessary and do not merit a reward; rather, our love of God will bring us closer to Christ.

14   As part of the monastic reform movement of Hildegard's era, lay sisters (and lay brothers) were introduced into religious communities to handle housekeeping chores and other manual labor so the choir nuns had more time for the Divine Office and study. Sometimes called "extern sisters," the lay sisters were full members of the community. This practice during the Middle Ages also gave working-class people an opportunity to participate in monastic life.

15   This letter was to a detractor, Tengswich, the head of a house of canonesses in Andernach, north of Bingen, in the Rhine Valley. (Canonesses were typically unenclosed women religious who lived a life of chastity and obedience, often following the Rule of St. Augustine.) Though Tengswich's letter, which prompted this response, is framed as a request for instruction, she is not a fan of Hildegard's, and in her letter accuses her of only allowing upper-class women into the Rupertsberg community and of following strange and unusual practices, such as having her nuns wear white garments with flowing hair and gems on feast days. Both accusations are true. But in this return letter, Hildegard goes further than justifying her position of leadership. Rather, she sets out to explain her practices, and in so doing offers an elaborate exposition on the glory of womanhood. It is astonishingly positive for the era, and it serves to balance some of her more conventional religious language in other texts. That this letter was possibly written even before the Rupertsberg convent was established indicates

Excessive abstinence leads to vanity and arrogance without foundation. It also produces much fearfulness, which may appear to be holy, but is not.

Those who practice this vanity are morally unstable, and become angry instead of peaceful. Let people who desire to have a kingly life while wearing a religious habit avoid luxurious banquets of rich foods that contribute to lust; let them avoid drinking strong wine lecherously and other unhealthy vices. But let virtuous people who love their souls eat food in proper moderation, and partake of wine that does not inflame with the fire of its own heat.[12]

What I give humankind to eat, I do not take away, but loathsome foods I do not recommend, because they are full of vanity. Let no one escape me through immoderate abstinence, for I will not receive them. Let them not strive and gnash their teeth for a reward that they have not earned through their practices. Rather, I give to all people a just reward according to their merits and to the extent that they love me.[13]

TO LAY SISTER JUTTA,[14] CA. 1143–1157; *EPISTOLARIUM* (LETTERS) 234

☐ Virginity and Greenness

The Living Fountain says: "Let a woman hide within her chamber and preserve her modesty, because the serpent breathed the fiery perils of horrible lust into her." Why should she do this?

Because the beauty of woman shines and blazes forth in the primal root, and in her is formed the part where every creature lies hidden. Why is she so resplendent? In two ways, first by being made by the finger of God and, second, because of her wondrous beauty. O woman, what a wonderful being you are, founded in the sun and conquering the earth.[15]

(continued on page 89)

Hildegard's popularity even outside her community. Some suggest that the inclusion of Tengswich's initial letter, and more importantly Hildegard's response, in Hildegard's collected letters stresses how she rose above her detractors.

In the opening paragraph, Hildegard affirms the need for women to safeguard their chastity, yet, unlike other contemporary authors, she does not stress women's weakness, but rather womanhood's incredible beauty. Not only is woman made by God, but she is also the source of life for all creatures.

16 In this section of the letter, Hildegard affirms the teachings of St. Paul, as she knew them, regarding the relationship between women and their husbands (2 Corinthians 12:2–4). Paul generally viewed relationships between husbands and wives as authoritarian: "Wives, submit yourselves unto your own husbands, as unto the Lord" (Ephesians 5:22 and Colossians 3:18). Interestingly, Hildegard tended to regard the role of the wife in more traditional terms than she did virgins. Paul often uses the metaphor of a "vessel" to refer to the body, and here Hildegard alludes to 1 Thessalonians 4:4–5: "Every one of you should know how to possess his vessel in sanctification and honor; not in the lust of concupiscence, even as the Gentiles which know not God."

17 This well-known phrase on the indissolubility of marriage is taken from the Gospel of Matthew 19:6.

18 The greenness that Hildegard refers to here is the universal life force that flows through creation. Its beauty is later covered up by winter. The life force is still there, but not for all eyes to see.

19 Hildegard argues that, indeed, a married woman ought not to adorn herself ostentatiously, unless her husband approves, and even then in moderation.

But the apostle Paul, who flew in the heights but was silent on earth, so that he would not reveal that which was hidden, observed this: A woman is subject to the power of her husband, joined to him through his first rib, and should have great modesty, by no means revealing her own vessel to another man who has no business with her, for that vessel belongs to her husband.[16] And let her do this in accordance with the word that the Lord of the earth declares in scorn of the Devil: "What God has joined together let no man put asunder."[17]

Listen: The earth keeps fresh greenness in the grass, until winter overtakes it.[18] Then winter takes away the beauty of that flower, and covers its vital force so it cannot reveal itself, as if it had never dried up, because winter spirits it away. So a woman, once married, should not overly adorn her hair, nor crown it with any diadem or gold ornament, unless her husband desires it, according to his pleasure, and even then in moderation.[19]

(continued on page 91)

20 By contrast, Hildegard argues that virgins are the powerful life force of the flowering branch. In Christian imagery, the Tree of Life is Christ, often depicted as an evergreen. For Hildegard, the virgin is a flowering branch of that tree. Also in Christian imagery, Christ as the evergreen is a symbol of eternal life. In prophetic literature the messiah is described as a branch, and his crucifixion as Christ "hung upon a tree."

21 But all these sanctions about dress do not pertain to virgins, argues Hildegard. Though many virgins cover their hair out of humility, they are not required to do so, as married women are, yet they do so in the same way as they hide the beauty of their souls, because the sin of pride would make them more vulnerable to evil influences. Theology professor Anne H. King-Lenzmeier notes that in writing on religious dress, Hildegard argued that others in church offices wore brightly colored attire, so why should nuns—virgins—be limited to a black veil and a cross? She thought that a white veil and tiara, or "circlet" in three colors, one for each person of the Trinity, was more appropriate in proclaiming the blessings they received from God (see *Hildegard of Bingen: An Integrated Vision* [Collegeville, MN: Liturgical Press, 2011], 77–78).

22 This paragraph of the letter asserts that virgins are "brides of Christ," and thus, it is perfectly acceptable for them to wear white dresses and veils, reasons Hildegard. The last two verses are apocryphal sayings that refer to the special status of virgins as those especially close to Christ.

But this does not apply to the virgin; she stands in the unsullied purity of paradise, beautiful and never dry, but she remains forever in the full greenness of the flowering branch.[20] A virgin is not commanded to cover her hair, but she covers it in greatest humility, for a person will naturally hide the beauty of her soul, lest, on account of pride, the hawk will carry it off.[21]

Virgins are married in the Holy Spirit, and in the bright dawn of virginity. And so it is proper that they come before the great High Priest as an offering dedicated to God. Thus, with the permission granted to her, and the revelation of the mystical vision of the finger of God, a virgin may be dressed in a white garment, a clear symbol of her marriage to Christ, considering that her mind is made one with the interwoven whole, and considering the One to whom she is married, as it is written: "Having his name and the name of his Father, written on their foreheads." And, again, "These follow the Lamb whithersoever he goeth."[22]

For it is God who keeps watch over every person, so that the lesser order does not rise above the higher, as did Satan and the first man, who wished to fly higher than their positions allowed. Now who would gather all his stock into one barn—oxen, asses, sheep, and kids? And so it is clear that separation is needed in this cases, lest people of various statuses, gathered in one flock, be scattered through the pride of their elevation, on the one hand, or the disgrace of their decline, on the other, and especially lest proper behavior should break down there, as they rend each other with hatred, as the highest order falls on the lower and when the lower gains ascendancy over the higher. For God ranks the people on earth as in heaven, as angels, archangels, thrones, dominions, cherubim, and seraphim. And they are all loved by God, but are not of equal rank. Pride loves princes and nobles for their elevated station, but hates them when they do away with it. And it is written, "God does not cast away the mighty because he himself was mighty." He does not love people for their rank, but for their works, which derives its

(continued on page 93)

23 Here Hildegard defends her practice of only accepting women of the highest socioeconomic ranks into her religious community. Monastic reformers such as the popular Cistercians, and canons and canonesses argued for the practice of opening the religious life to those of the poorer classes as well. This is one area where Hildegard was more conservative than many of her peers. When she did comment on people from lower classes, it was clearly from observation, rather than direct experience. In Hildegard's worldview, even those in heaven, like the angels, were ranked, and while the Divine did not love any one rank more than another, God clearly approved of keeping the ranks separate. Interestingly, the issue is important enough to Hildegard for her to contend that God does, indeed, love the rich, too, even though the Gospels clearly argue that God favors the poor. In arguing that God does not cast off the mighty, she is quoting from Job 36:5: "Behold, God is mighty, and despiseth not any..." The quotation "My food is to do the will of my Father" is taken from the Gospel of John 4:34.

24 The letter ends with Hildegard advising that it is not good for people to strive for higher things that are unattainable, but rather, to stay in their place and gain understanding. She also asserts that the Living Light is the true author of the letter.

savor from him, just as the Son of God says, "My food is to do the will of my Father." Where humanity is found, there Christ always prepares a feast, and so it is necessary that those who seek empty honor rather than humanity are identified, so they are assigned their proper place. Let the sick sheep be cast out lest the whole flock be contaminated.[23]

God has infused human beings with good understanding so that their name will not perish. For it is good that people do not seize a mountain that cannot be moved, but stay in the valley, gradually learning what they can understand. These words come from the Living Light and not from any person. Let them who hear, see and believe where these words come from.[24]

To Canoness Tengswich of Andernach, ca. 1148–1150,
possibly as late as 1170; *Epistolarium* (Letters) 52

Part 7
God's Creation

Hildegard upholds the importance of the created world in her spirituality, and accords humanity a special role within it. That is, humanity is made in the image of God from the dust of the earth, embraced by God throughout eternity, and the mediators of creation. Given bodies by the Creator, humankind has the world at its command. At the same time, Hildegard reminds humankind that God loves all creatures, and they are not to be abused or exploited; creation is not to be used by humanity, but rather, to be served by it. Hildegard is one of comparatively few medieval writers to reject negative attitudes toward the natural world. She does not see the world as inherently corrupt or evil, but believes that God's creative energy animates all things. For Hildegard, the natural world is not something to be avoided or to be conquered. Rather, it is filled with plants, animals, humans, stones, reptiles, birds, fish, and even unicorns, all of which are imbued with sacred mysteries. All of creation, even the stones under our feet, honors the Creator, and has a true purpose ordained by God.

1   In this text, Hildegard explains the relationship between humanity and other creatures. In her cosmology, humanity, despite its privileged place in the hierarchy of creation, is not distinct from other creatures, though she believes that it is the role of redeemed humanity to take the place of fallen angels. Still, Hildegard reasons, humans are meant to respect and care for other creatures appropriately. Although Hildegard is aware of humanity's shortcomings, and insists that we need to be redeemed by the saving action of Christ, overall she views creation and humans' role in it as divinely inspired and, therefore, good. The goal, she believes, is to achieve harmony between created beings, including humanity and other creatures.

2   Hildegard understands humanity as the heart in the center of an interdependent creation, because humanity is made in the image of God. Just as we see all God's creatures with our bodily eyes, so too can those who have faith see God in all of creation. This text is from the second vision in Hildegard's *Liber divinorum operum.* In this vision of the wheel with a human being at its center, God encompasses the circle. The human figure shows that humanity is at the center of creation and has a special relationship to all created things. An underlying message of the vision is the love God has for all creation.

☐ Humanity and Other Creatures

Once again I heard a voice from heaven that said this to me: God has commanded for humanity's benefit all of creation, which God made on the heights and in the depths. If humanity abuses their position over the rest of God's creation and commits evil deeds, God will then allow other creatures to punish us. Other creatures are not here just to serve our bodily needs. If we appreciate them as God intended, our souls will benefit.[1]

LIBER DIVINORUM OPERUM (BOOK OF THE DIVINE WORKS) 3.2

☐ Humanity as Microcosm

In the middle of this wheel appears the figure of a human person.[2] The top of its head extends upward, while the soles of its feet extend downward against a circle that is white and shining air. From the right side the fingertips of the right hand and on the left the fingertips of the left hand are extended to the circle, both of them toward this vision of light, as if the figure stretched out its arms. This has the following message:

Humanity stands at the center of the world. For it is more important than the rest of the creatures dependent on the world. Though small in stature, humankind is great in strength of its soul. Its head turns upward and its feet are solid on the ground, and it can put into motion elements both higher and lower. Whatever it does with its actions to the right and left hand permeates the universe, because the power that comes from the inner strength of the person can accomplish such things. For as a person's body exceeds the heart in size, so also the strength of the soul exceeds the strength of the body. As the heart of a human being is hidden in the body, so also is the body surrounded by the powers of the soul, which extend throughout the entire world. The faithful live in

(continued on page 99)

3 From Genesis 1:26: "And God said, Let us make man in our image, after our likeness: and let them have dominion over the fish of the sea, and over the fowl of the air, and over the cattle, and over all the earth, and over every creeping thing that creepeth upon the earth."

4 Among medieval Platonists it was common to depict the empirical world as a "shadow," or reflection, of the authentic life of creatures in the mind of God (see Newman, *Sister of Wisdom*, 51).

5 This excerpt is from Hildegard's larger text on the infusion of the soul, which occurs a few months after conception in the womb. For Hildegard, humanity is the mirror of all God's miracles, and the whole celestial harmony reflects divinity. Mirrors are often used as a metaphor for celestial hierarchy.

the knowledge of God, and turn to God in their spiritual and worldly endeavors. Whether good progress is made in these undertakings, or whether they do not succeed, those people always direct their devotions to God since, in both situations, they ceaselessly express their awe. For as people see creatures everywhere with their bodily eyes, so they see God everywhere in faith. It is God whom human beings know through every creature. For they know that God is the creator of the whole world.

LIBER DIVINORUM OPERUM (BOOK OF THE DIVINE WORKS) 1.2.15

☐ Mirror of Divinity

Thus God and the human are one, as the soul and the body are one, because human beings are made in the image of God.[3] Everything has its shadow, so too humanity is the shadow of God, and this shadow is the manifestation of all creation.[4] Humanity is thus the manifestation of all God's miracles. The human being is in itself a shadow because it has a beginning. God has neither a beginning nor an end. Thus the whole celestial harmony is the mirror of divinity, and humanity is the mirror of all God's miracles.[5]

CAUSE ET CURE (CAUSE AND CURE) 4

6 Over the course of her writings, Hildegard refers to predestination, which, in her interpretation, is the existence of all creatures in the world within the heart and mind of God before time began.

7 This tender antiphon to God the Creator tells the story of the creation of humankind—how God gazed into the face of humanity in Adam and saw the culmination of all creation. Hildegard's sense of the order of creation is hierarchical, with humanity as the highest level of earthly being, made in God's image. To Hildegard, humanity is the place where creation unites with God, through Jesus Christ, the Redeemer.

8 Hildegard experienced this imagery as part of a larger vision of the structure of the universe. The cosmic egg is a layered and structured Aristotelian vision of the universe, or cosmos, sometimes also depicted in the Middle Ages as a series of nested spheres with the earth at the center, and was based on astrological understandings of her time. As a symbol there is a unity to an egg, as well as a sense of anticipation, and of making something new.

Although the image of the cosmic egg is not original to Hildegard, she develops it as a symbol of the earth, surrounded by divine fire. The egg is a metaphor for the world and the church: The yolk of the egg is the earth, the surrounding white is ether or air, and the shell that encases the egg is the firmament. The universe is created, nurtured, and held in the womb of God.

9 The outermost layer of the egg is a ring of fire, which holds the universe together and also serves as a symbol of purification. This outer layer of flame is dynamic and surrounded by an inner darkness of struggle. The earth is suspended in the middle of the egg and surrounded by virtues that resemble sparkling stars.

☐ O How Miraculous

O how miraculous is
the foresight of the divine heart,
that foretold every creature.[6]
For when God gazed
upon the face of the human being he had formed
he saw the entirety of all his works
in that same human form.
O how miraculous is the breath
that awakened humankind to life.[7]

SYMPHONIA (SONGS) 3

☐ The Cosmic Egg

After this I saw a vast object, round and shady. It was shaped like an egg: pointed on the top, wide in the middle, and narrower on the bottom.[8] On its outer layer there was an aura of bright fire with a dark layer beneath it. In that outer layer there was red fire so brilliant that the entire globe was lit up by it. Above the fireball was a vertical row of three torches that prevented the fire from falling on the globe itself. At times, the fireball shot upwards and was met by more fire, which caused it to shoot out great long flames. At times, the fireball moved downwards and encountered a great coldness that caused it to quickly retract its flames. From the outer layer of fire, a blast blew whirlwinds.[9] And from the dark layer underneath, another wind raged with further turbulence, which moved out in all directions of the globe. The dark layer also contained a shadowy fire of such horror that I was unable to look at it properly. The shadowy fire was shaking the dark layers with a great force of thunder, storms, and sharp stones, large and small.

(continued on page 103)

10 Here Hildegard uses the image of ether—a highly flammable liquid or, in the figurative sense, the air above the clouds—to symbolize faith or belief.

11 These are images of the sun (red fireball), the moon (white fireball), and the stars (many white spheres). The sun is a Christ symbol, as he is considered the sun of justice; the moon represents the church, which reflects the light of Christ; and the stars symbolize works of devotion.

12 The image of water that spreads throughout the world symbolizes baptism.

Whenever the thunders arose, that set in motion the layers of bright fire, winds, and air, thus causing bolts of lightning to precede the sounds of thunder. The fire on the outer edge understood the turbulence of the thunder.

Under the dark layer was the purest ether, with no layer beneath it.[10] Here I saw a white fireball of great magnitude; it had two torches placed above, which prevented it from passing beyond its course. Scattered everywhere throughout the ether were many bright spheres, into which the white fireball poured itself out at regular intervals. It then rose up again to the red fireball, where it renewed its flames and sent them out again into the bright spheres.[11] The ether also contained a blast of wind, which spread itself out over the cosmos. Beneath the ether I could see a layer of watery air, which had a white layer. It spread out everywhere, giving off moisture to the whole of the world.[12] At times it accumulated quickly and sent out a sudden rain with a great deal of thunder; when it spread itself out again, it sent forth a gentle, soft rain. But from it, too, came a whirlwind that spread storms all over the globe. In the middle of this air there was a dry globe of a very large size, which was so surrounded that it could not move in any direction. However, when the winds shook the air, the force set the whole world in motion with its strength. And between the north and the east of the dry globe, I saw a great mountain, which to the north showed areas of great darkness, and toward the east had great light. But darkness could not reach the light, nor could the light reach the darkness.

Scivias (Know the Ways of the Lord) 1.3

13 This text is a good example of how Hildegard's scientific writing and her theological writing merged. Elsewhere, she writes about the position of the sun and the moon and the stars in the firmament, with, of course, the sun at its center. Here she adds a further dimension to her cosmology, and her vision of the church. This text comes after Hildegard explains a vision of *ecclesia*, the church, clothed in the glory of many colors: crystal to symbolize the priesthood, rose for virginity, purple for monastics, and a "cloudy brightness" for secular people. There, in her reflections on this vision, Hildegard uses the sun, the moon, and the stars to symbolize the church: The sun at the center symbolizes Christ, the moon is emblematic of the church, and the stars, the members of monastic orders.

14 Like many devout people of her day, Hildegard was deeply suspicious of people who were not Christians, believing their interest was to undermine the church. There was limited appreciation among Christians that Judaism or Islam had integrity as faith traditions on their own. Though Hildegard could at times show deep compassion to excluded persons, she also exhibited the prejudices of her era. Elsewhere in this letter, she includes the clause "whether bad Christians, Jews, or pagans."

15 Here Hildegard comments on the church of her era, of which she was both supportive and critical. She thought that many of the church leaders of her day were less than impressive, and often more concerned with secular affairs than the word of God.

16 Unlike the Platonic worldview, which separates the soul from the body, Hildegard asserts that the soul, the body, and the senses are interconnected and interdependent. Throughout her writing, Hildegard stresses the importance of the integration of the body and the soul.

☐ The Sun, Moon, and Stars

From the splendor I heard a voice saying: These are great mysteries. Consider the sun, the moon, and the stars. I created the sun to light the day and the moon and the stars to light the night. The sun signifies my Son, who was born from my heart and illuminated the world, when, at the end of the ages, he was born of the Virgin, as the sun shines forth, rising at the end of the night, and lighting up the world.[13]

The moon symbolizes the church, betrothed to my Son in a heavenly marriage. As the moon, according to its nature, is always increasing and decreasing, not shining by its own power but kindled by the light of the sun, so too does the church also go through stages. She increases when her children grow in virtue, and wanes through their deviant behavior or destructive forces against her. For it happens frequently that she is attacked in her mysteries by thieving wolves, that is, evil people.[14] She is not kindled with the power to resist from within herself but from me through my Son to persevere in the good.

The stars differ considerably from each other in their power to shine. They symbolize the people of the various religious orders of the church.[15]

SCIVIAS (KNOW THE WAYS OF THE LORD) 2.5

☐ Three Paths

A human being contains three paths: namely, the soul, the body, and the senses.[16] All human life runs its course in these paths. The soul fills the body and brings forth the breath of life to the senses; the body draws the soul to itself and opens the senses; and the senses touch the soul and draw the body to themselves. The soul gives life to the body as fire gives light to darkness; it has two principal powers like two arms:

(continued on page 107)

17 Here Hildegard is saying that human beings should be aware that they are more than bodies and should pay more attention to all the paths that constitute human life, including the soul and the senses.

18 This excerpt is from a letter to Abbot Ludwig (d. 1187), a close friend and major supporter of Hildegard's. He was abbot of St. Eucharius in Trier from 1168 to 1173, when he resigned to become abbot of Echternach, a Benedictine monastery in what is now eastern Luxembourg. Ludwig was instrumental in commissioning Theodoric of Echternach to complete Hildegard's *Vita.* She trusted him to the extent that she accepted his help in editing the *Liber divinorum.* Ludwig served as her secretary for a short time after Volmar's death in 1173.

This excerpt spells out Hildegard's view on the evolution of humanity, from the creation story through the human life cycle. Though she begins the letter with her theological account of God breathing life into humankind, she later offers a more observational perspective on the human life cycle.

19 Hildegard develops a sense of the human life cycle that runs parallel to the hours of the day, beginning with the first hour, which is in darkness. The hours correspond with the hours Jesus Christ hung on the cross. For instance, he hung on the cross during the third hour; darkness covered the land during the sixth hour; and he died at the ninth hour.

the intellect and the will. The soul has these arms not to move herself about; rather she reveals herself in these two powers as the sun reveals itself in the brilliance of its light. Therefore, human being, you are not a bundle of marrow; pay attention to the knowledge of the Scriptures.[17]

SCIVIAS (KNOW THE WAYS OF THE LORD) 1.4.18

☐ The Human Life Cycle

The sun rises in the morning and from its place in the sky it permeates all the clouds with its light like a mirror, and it rules and illuminates all creatures with its heat until evening. In this way, God fashioned all creation, which is humankind, and afterward animated and illuminated it with the breath of life.[18]

Just as the morning begins with damp cold and shifting clouds, so humanity in infancy is damp and cold, because the body is growing and the bones are not yet full of marrow, and the blood does not yet have its full strength. As the third hour begins to grow warm with the course of the sun, so the person begins to consume food and learns to walk.

In youth when childhood is over, people become bold, happy, and carefree, and begin to think about what they might do in life. If by the light of the sun they choose the good by turning to the right, they will become productive and a source of good works. But if they turn to the left and choose evil, they will become evil and corrupt in sin. When they reach the ninth hour by doing their work, they become arid and weary in flesh and bone and the other powers through which they grew and developed. So the great Artisan set in order the ages of the world from the first hour to the evening.[19]

(continued on page 109)

20 In Hildegard's age, people generally believed in unicorns, though they never actually caught one. Unicorn horns were considered to have powerful healing properties and were expensive. (They were actually narwhal whale tusks.) In terms of Christian iconography, the unicorn is associated with virginity, because unicorns can only be tamed by virgins, and the unicorn is a symbol of Jesus Christ. Here Hildegard suggests that her friend was seeking God before he was even aware of it.

21 In this excerpt from another letter to Abbot Ludwig, Hildegard explains people's basic "temperaments," or dispositions, observing that they are all found in humanity, none being more valuable than another, and all created from a single breath of God. Here the implication is that balance in these four humors is important. Later in the letter Hildegard explains that the humors in the abbot's community are out of balance with his own; hence they are in conflict.

22 Always concerned with clergy and religious who put their secular ambitions before their ministry, Hildegard discusses in this paragraph the impact of various temperaments, ending with a condemnation of those whose secular ambitions even cause them to resort to violence.

O father, you take your name from the Father, therefore reflect on your origins and how your life has proceeded, for in your childhood you lacked wisdom, and in your youth you were happy and carefree. In the meantime, however, unbeknownst to yourself, you were seeking the affairs of the unicorn.[20]

To Abbot Ludwig of Echternach, ca. 1173–1174; *Epistolarium* (Letters) 217

☐ Human Temperaments

The hidden mysteries of God cannot be understood or known by those things that came forth at the beginning. Yet, all God's judgments are just; there is no need in God, for just as God was, God is now. Just as a human being is formed by the elements, and the elements are joined into one, with none being of value without the other, so too there are various temperaments of humankind, though all come to light from a single breath.[21]

The temperaments of humankind exist in four humors: hard, airy, stormy, fiery. People who are hard are embittered in every part of their life. They conduct all their affairs alone, consulting with no one. The mind of those who are airy is always wavering, and thus they show prudence in their sins because they fear God and are dissatisfied with their actions. The stormy are foolish, and they act in a misguided way in all they do. They are not taught by words of wisdom, but shudder at them with resentment. Lastly, those who are fiery distance themselves from that which is spiritual and devote their attention to the secular. Their secular ambition does violence to peace, and they reject peace wherever they see it.

But God gathers people of all temperaments to himself when they come to understand those things that are contrary to their salvation and turn back to God, as Saul did.[22]

To Abbot Ludwig of Echternach, ca. 1173; *Epistolarium* (Letters) 216

Part 8
Celestial Harmony

Hildegard's theology of music is closely associated with her view of celestial harmony. For Hildegard, music is an integral component of her spirituality. All music, and the arts in general, are divinely inspired, in Hildegard's view. As a Benedictine nun, many of her waking hours were devoted to liturgy and music, and thus, her musical compositions spring from her passion for musical expression. Hildegard envisions the whole cosmos in musical terms; that is, as a musical composition, reverberating through the universe. Every element has its own sound, and all the tones blend into a universal harmony. All those in celestial harmony are united in praising God. Though angels have the advantage of singing God's praises for all eternity, humanity, too, has the capacity to praise God, and in music finds the closest experience of celestial harmony this side of heaven.

~ Barbara Newman, in *Symphonia* (page 177), notes that this sequence is considered one of Hildegard's finest pieces. Newman also points out that after Hildegard's death, three of her nuns testified that they saw her chanting this sequence through the cloister, illuminated by the Holy Spirit. Not only is it an artful hymn to the Virgin Mary, but it is also an example of Hildegard's use of the term *celestial harmony*. For Hildegard, the entire cosmos is a well-tuned musical composition. In a sense, the entire history of salvation, from a Christian perspective, ends in celestial harmony; it is also the sound that resounds in the human soul. The songs human beings sing in praise of God are an echo of this same celestial harmony.

1 In this section Hildegard contrasts the natural birth of offspring, through Adam, and the incarnation.

2 Hildegard writes of the Virgin Mary as the "matrix of sanctity," using "matrix" as another term for womb, for out of her womb all the harmonies of heaven resounded.

3 In Hildegard's theology of music, angels sing out God's praise for all eternity.

4 Here Hildegard recalls how, through the sin of Eve, all women are implicated in sin, until they are redeemed by the Virgin Mary.

☐ For the Virgin Mary

O branch and diadem of royal purple,
in your cloister like a breastplate,
you grew leaves and flowered in another way
from that which Adam begot the human race.
Hail, hail![1]

Out of your womb came forth another life,
that which Adam stripped from his children.
Flower, you did not spring from the dew
or drops of rain, nor did the breeze fly over you,
but divine radiance brought you forth on the noblest branch.

O branch, your flowering
foreseen by God on the first day
of creation:
Out of his Word he made of you a golden matrix[2]
O Virgin destined for praise!

How great in its strength is the man's side,
from which God brought forth woman,
making her the mirror of all beauty,
and the embrace of all creation.

Heavenly instruments make harmony[3]
and all the earth marvels, O Mary,
destined for praise,
for God loved you greatly.

O how must we mourn and lament
because, at the serpent's persuasion,
sadness flowed with guilt into woman.[4]

(continued on page 115)

5 Through Mary's role in the history of salvation, Eve's sin in the Garden of Eden is reversed.

6 The music of creation is born from a virgin's womb, and now the whole creation rejoices and unites in celestial harmony. Hildegard believes Mary is the one who made the salvation of humankind possible, and she is referred to here as a female savior.

7 This brief text is part of the last vision in *Scivias*, which is dedicated to the power of music. Hildegard defines liturgical music as that which unites the body, spirit, and celestial harmony in Christ. Anne H. King-Lenzmeier writes about the connections Hildegard made between heaven and music: the link between the Incarnation as the embodiment of the Spirit in the church and the connection between the body and soul in paradise are made apparent in music. Through music heaven and earth come in contact, serving as a way for a religious community to be aware of their humanity in the world and their destiny in heaven (see *Hildegard of Bingen: An Integrated Vision*, 81–83).

For that woman whom God made
to be the mother of all
lacerated her womb with the wounds of ignorance
and bore the fullness of pain for her kind.

But from your womb, O dawn,
a new sun came forth
that cleansed all of Eve's guilt
and, through you, brought a blessing
for humankind greater than Eve's harm.[5]

O Saving Lady,
You who bore the new light
for humankind,
Gather up the members of your Son
into celestial harmony.[6]

Symphonia (Songs) 20

☐ Jubilant Music

So the words symbolize the body; the jubilant music shows the spirit; thus the celestial harmony reflects the divinity and the words the humanity of the Son of God. The words are his body, symbolizing his humanity, while the music symbolizes his spirit and divinity.[7]

Scivias (Know the Ways of the Lord) 3.13.12

8 Here *ecclesia* is the female image for the universal church. The word is a Latin term from the Greek, meaning "gathering" or "assembly." Before the word became equivalent to "church," it referred to the idea of a people or a community receiving wisdom. In the ancient and medieval worlds, blue sapphires were symbols of the heavens, wisdom, and royalty. Both Solomon and Abraham wore talismans of sapphire, and the tablets of the law received by Moses were said to be made of sapphire.

9 Mount Bethel, a town and an important worship center (literally, "house of God"), is located north of Jerusalem where Abraham offered his sacrifice on his way south to Shechem.

10 This refers to the Song of Songs, where the lover awaits his bride in fragrant places.

11 This mystical poem, often referred to as Hildegard's most famous hymn, is set to music to recount the martyrdom of St. Ursula and her 11,000 virgin companions. Ursula, one of the saints most admired by Hildegard, was at the center of a popular medieval cult. The hymn is called a sequence, but it does not conform to the musical conventions of the time, more closely resembling Hildegard's free-form songs. Beyond the events focused on the life of Ursula and her companions, the hymn is a wider celebration of virginity and erotic mysticism.

St. Ursula was probably not a historical figure, and the date of the martyrdom of St. Ursula and her companions is not recorded, though an inscription (ca. 400) in the Church of St. Ursula at Cologne states that a ruined church was restored there in honor of local virgin martyrs. Early accounts from the eighth and ninth centuries list her companions as five, eight, and eleven virgin martyrs; this number expanded to eleven thousand by the tenth century (probably due to an inaccurate translation of a text). Once launched, the cult grew in popularity quickly. A popular version of this story features Ursula as a British Christian princess, engaged to a pagan prince. She was able to obtain a three-year delay of the marriage because she wished to remain a

☐ O Church (of 11,000 Virgins)

O Church,[8]
your eyes are like sapphires;
your ears are like Mount Bethel;[9]
your nose is like a mountain of incense and myrrh,[10]
and your mouth is like the sound of many waters.

In a vision of true faith,
Ursula loved the Son of God,[11]
rejected a husband and the world alike,
gazed toward the sun
and called to the most beautiful youth,
saying:

In great yearning I have longed
to come to you
and sit with you at the heavenly wedding feast,
running to you by a new path
like a cloud that,
in the purest sky,
races like sapphire.

And after Ursula had said thus,
this report spread among the people.
And they said:
In the innocence of girlish ignorance
she knows not what she is saying.

(continued on page 119)

virgin. She spent this time on a ship, traveling to Cologne, Basel, and on pilgrimage to Rome, accompanied by ten virgin companions, each with a ship with a thousand more companions. Upon their return to Cologne, they were martyred by the Huns for their Christian faith, and for Ursula's refusal to marry their prince, and buried there. In 1106 a large collection of bones was unearthed in Cologne, and even though the relics included the remains of men and children, they were proclaimed the bones of Ursula and her followers. Accounts of Ursula and her eleven thousand followers inspired not only Hildegard but also another German Benedictine mystic, Elisabeth of Schönau (1126–1165), who wrote *Revelations Concerning the Sacred Army of Virgins of Cologne.*

12 As the story goes, Ursula and her companions were mocked by their captors. As Ursula is martyred, she is unified with the church.

13 This word is a German exclamation of dismay, inserted into the Latin text.

14 Through the martyrdom of St. Ursula and her companions, all of creation rejoices in celestial harmony. The Devil is "strangled," and all of heaven unites in praise of God.

And they began to mock her
in a great chorus
until the fiery burden
fell upon her.[12]

Then all people knew
that contempt for the world is
like Mount Bethel.

And they knew also
the sweetest fragrance
of incense and myrrh
because contempt for the world
rises over all things.

Then the Devil
inspired those who were his own,
who, in those bodies,
slaughtered the noblest way of life.

All the elements that heard this deed,
and cried out
before the throne of God, said:

Ach![13]
The scarlet blood of an innocent lamb
is poured out at her betrothal:
Let all the heavens hear this
and, in the celestial harmony,
praise the lamb of God:
for the throat of the ancient serpent
is strangled in these pearls
formed from the Word of God.[14]

Symphonia (Songs) 64

15 These texts on the power of music are taken from the last section of the *Scivias* and follow fourteen songs composed by Hildegard, plus a lament, a prayer of intercession for the fallen, and a play.

16 The word *consonance* is used here in its musical sense—that is, a combination of notes that are in harmony with each other due to the relationship between their frequencies. This experience of music is the closest humans get to heaven while on earth.

17 Here Hildegard writes that music is transcendent, for song passes through the body, to a place of pureness and light, surpassing all weaknesses of the flesh.

18 From Psalm 150: "Praise him with the sound of the trumpet: praise him with the psaltery and harp.... Let everything that hath breath praise the Lord."

19 These texts are excerpted from a letter alluding to a bitter controversy that affected Hildegard and her nuns near the end of her life, when she was eighty years old. In 1178, Hildegard permitted the burial of a nobleman in the cemetery at St. Rupertsberg. The deceased had at one time been excommunicated, and while Hildegard believed he had reconciled with the church before his death, the prelates of Mainz ordered her to exhume the body and remove it from holy ground, under pain of excommunication herself. There is some suspicion cast

☐ Song of Rejoicing

As the power of God is everywhere and encompasses all things so nothing can resist it, so too the human mind has great power to resound in living voices and arouse sluggish souls to watchfulness by a song....[15]

For the song of rejoicing softens hardened hearts, leads to tears of reconciliation, and invokes the Holy Spirit. Those voices you hear and the voices of a multitude, lifting its sound on high, jubilant praises offered in simple harmony and love, lead the faithful to the consonance where there is no discord, and make those who still live on earth yearn with heart and voice for their heaven.[16]

And the sound of these voices passes through you so that you understand perfectly. For wherever divine grace has worked, it casts out all the shadows of darkness, and makes pure and light those things that have been obscured by the bodily senses in the weakness of the flesh.[17]

SCIVIAS (KNOW THE WAYS OF THE LORD) 3.13.13–14

☐ Music and the Prophetic Spirit

And I heard a voice coming from the Living Light about the kinds of praises that David speaks about in the psalm: "Praise him with the sound of a trumpet; Praise him with psaltery and harp," and so forth, up to the following point: "Let every spirit praise the Lord."[18] These words are outward, visible signs to teach us about invisible things.[19] The composition and the quality of these instruments teach us how we ought to praise the Creator and turn all convictions of our innermost being to the same. When we consider these things, we remember that humankind needs the voice of the living Spirit, but Adam lost his voice because of his disobedience. Before his transgression, while he was still innocent,

(continued on page 123)

over the high-ranking clergy's actions, as they were insisting that the orders be carried out quickly, while the archbishop was away in Rome. Convinced of the dead man's innocence, Hildegard refused to obey the order. Hence, Rupertsberg was placed under interdict, and the nuns forbidden to sing the Divine Office or to celebrate the Mass. Hildegard and her community experienced the loss of music deeply. This letter was sent by Hildegard to the clergy of Mainz in response to the interdict, and is framed as a vision from "God the Great Artisan." In the letter, Hildegard discusses her theory of music. The bishops did not lift the interdict, causing Hildegard to appeal to higher-placed friends.

[20] Hildegard makes the argument that a scriptural mandate calls for humankind to serenade the Creator with music.

[21] Hildegard argues that music is the one way for humanity, body and soul, to incarnate heaven. In doing so, humanity participates in the celestial harmony with the angels.

[22] Again, a reference to Psalm 150, this time from verse 5: "Praise him upon the loud cymbals: praise him upon the high sounding cymbals."

[23] Hildegard describes all the arts as the breath of God flowing through the human body; creativity is a sign of the Holy Spirit.

[24] Hildegard makes the powerful statement that the "soul is symphonic," or the soul is like music, or a harmony of sounds.

[25] From Psalm 92:3: "Upon an instrument of ten strings, and upon the psaltery; upon the harp with a solemn sound."

[26] In this paragraph Hildegard warns that those who unjustly deprive the faithful of music will not only be punished, but they will also lose their own place in heaven.

his voice blended fully with the voices of the angels in their praise of God.[20]...

Consider as well, that just as the body of Jesus Christ was born of the pure Virgin Mary through the inspiration of the Holy Spirit, so too is the canticle of praise, reflecting celestial harmony, rooted in the church through the Holy Spirit. The body is the vestment of the spirit, which has a living voice, and thus it is appropriate for the body in harmony with the soul to use its voice to sing the praises of God.[21] Therefore, according to the metaphor, it is the command of the prophetic spirit for us to praise God with clashing cymbals and the cymbals of jubilation,[22] as well as with other musical instruments that people of wisdom and religious zeal have embraced, because all the arts pertaining to that which is necessary and useful for humankind have been created by the breath of God, sent into the human body. Therefore it is proper that God be praised in all things.[23]

Because sometimes a person sighs and groans while singing, remembering the nature of celestial harmony, the prophet, aware that the soul is symphonic[24] and reflecting on the profound nature of the spirit, urges us through the psalm to confess to the Lord with the harp, and to sing a psalm to him with the ten-stringed psaltery.[25] This means that the harp, plucked from below, is akin to the discipline of the body; the psaltery, which is plucked from above, reflects the exertion of the spirit; the ten chords echo the fulfillment of the law.

Therefore, those who impose silences on a church without just cause, and prohibit the singing of God's praises, and those who have unjustly despoiled God on earth, will lose their place among the chorus of angels unless, through true penitence and humble restitution, they have amended their lives. Also, let those who hold the keys of heaven beware not to open those things which are to be kept closed or to close those things which are to be kept open, for harsh judgment will fall upon those who rule, unless they rule, the apostle says, with good judgment.[26]...

(continued on page 125)

27 The term *womanish* is used by Hildegard throughout her works. She means that the church in her time has lost its "virility," and she feels that the clergy are being replaced by those she calls "weak and effeminate" creatures. Critical of the clergy in her time, Hildegard believed that many had lost their moral stature and their ability to command the respect of the people. Against simony, and for clerical celibacy, Hildegard found the church of her day morally lax, compared to the early church. It is with irony that she then argues that God sent a woman warrior to help the church reclaim its virility.

28 In this first paragraph, Hildegard focuses on music as an expression of the prophetic voice, through the aid of musical instruments. Through the acts of singing and playing musical instruments, people cultivate their inner spiritual lives, reaching beyond the outer world. In this way, the prophets, through the psalms and canticles, participate in the kind of heavenly music that humanity knew before the Fall.

29 In this second section, Hildegard likens the playing of musical instruments with human fingers to God's creative activity when he made humanity. Before the Fall, according to medieval tradition, Adam had a voice so beautiful that sinful mortals would not be able to tolerate it.

This time is a womanish time because the dispensation of God's justice is weak. But the strength of God's justice is exerting itself, a female warrior battling against injustice, so it might be defeated.[27]

TO THE BISHOPS AT MAINZ, CA. 1178–1179; EPISTOLARIUM (LETTERS) 23

☐ Musical Instruments

So the holy prophets, inspired by the Spirit they had received, were called for this purpose; not only to compose psalms and canticles (through which the hearts of listeners would be uplifted) but also to make various kinds of musical instruments to enrich these songs of praise with melodic lines. Both through the design and the quality of the instruments, as well as through the message of the words that accompany them, those who hear are taught about inward things, since they have been enticed by outward things. In this way, the holy prophets, in the company of angels, go beyond the music of this exile and recollect the divine melody of praise that Adam delighted in before his Fall.[28]

People of devotion and wisdom have imitated the holy prophets and have themselves, with human skills, created several kinds of musical instruments, so that they might be able to sing for the delight of their souls, and accompany their singing with instruments played by the flexing of fingers. In this way, they recall Adam, created by God's finger. Before he sinned, his voice had the beauty of all musical harmony. Indeed, if Adam had remained in his original state, sinful mortals would not be able to bear the intensity and sonority of his voice.[29]

TO THE BISHOPS AT MAINZ, CA. 1178–1179, EPISTOLARIUM (LETTERS) 23

Part 9
Healing Sciences

The Benedictine Order has a long history in the healing arts and founded one of the first institutions in the Middle Ages for the care of the sick and the infirm. Hildegard, too, was trained as a healer. Though we do not know the extent of her training or the academic sources she used to ground her work, she is clearly familiar with the medicine and science of her era. Her medical and scientific works are pragmatic and practical; overall, she advocates a life of moderation and respect for all of creation. Hildegard stresses that disease is a symptom of humankind's Fall from grace. Her scientific views are based on humoral medicine and the ancient Greek cosmology of the four elements—fire, air, water, and earth—with their four qualities of heat, dryness, moisture, and cold. In this schema, the body is also made up of four humors: choler (yellow bile), blood, phlegm, and melancholia (black bile). Illness upsets the balance of the humors of the body, and the goal of medicine is to restore balance to the body. In addition to healing practices, Hildegard understood the basic science of plants, animals, birds, elements, stones, and the like, and was familiar with their healing properties and their uses in treating a wide variety of diseases.

1 Hildegard believed that sleep was an essential human need to restore the body. Her view of dreams followed popular beliefs rooted in antiquity. That is, while the body is asleep, the soul is awake; the soul works independently of the body, and it can see the future when the body is asleep. Here Hildegard does not describe the origins of dreams, but rather she makes the point that unresolved problems and desires find their way into dreams.

2 In the last two sentences of the text, Hildegard states that if people's thoughts are good, they are able to prophesy and have visions in their sleep. Nightmares occur when a person's thoughts are bad; the Devil also torments people in sleep.

3 Hildegard believed in eating and drinking in moderation, and was supported in this assertion by the Rule of St. Benedict. She advises lighter and more frequent meals for children and the aged. Hildegard considers both wine and beer strengthening.

4 Concerns about water purity made people in the Middle Ages suspicious of drinking water. Upper-class people, like Hildegard, were also concerned that drinking water carried with it a lack of prestige. Most people received their water intake from food and other drinks.

☐ Dreams

Since the human soul is from God, sometimes sleeping people can see true and future things while the body is asleep.[1] Then they learn future things that sometimes do occur. It often happens, too, that the soul, disturbed by a devilish illusion or overburdened by mental turmoil, cannot with certainty see or understand these events. For it is often the case that people are weighed down in their sleep by the thoughts and opinions and aspirations that occupied them while awake. At times, depending on whether these thoughts are good or evil, they are lifted up in sleep like a batch of dough. If the thoughts are honorable and holy, then God's grace often shows a person something true in sleep. However, if the thoughts are arrogant, the Devil sees it and torments the soul and mixes his lies into the person's thoughts.[2]

CAUSE ET CURE (CAUSE AND CURE) 7

☐ Food and Drink

If land rich in grain produces wine, this is healthier to the sick than wine made from fruit-bearing land; that is, land that produces a moderate amount of grain, although it costs more. Wine heals and makes people happy with its wholesome heat and curative powers.

Beer puts flesh on the bones and gives a lovely color to the face, because of the strength and wholesome juices of the grain. Water has a weakening effect, and for the sick sometimes causes bad humors in the lungs, since water is weak and has no qualities of strength. But if a person is healthy and drinks water in moderation, it will do no harm.[3]

Whether people are healthy or sick, they are thirsty after sleeping. They should drink wine or beer, not water, because water might damage, rather than support, a person's blood and humors.[4]

(continued on page 131)

5 Consistent with the advice here, the Benedictine Rule provides for one main meal of the day, eaten at around noon, and then a lighter supper in the evening. Hildegard believed in giving more red meat to the sick, though the Rule forbids its consumption by the healthy.

6 The griffin is an animal that exists in legend only. It has the body, tail, and back legs of a lion, and the head and wings of an eagle, with talons on its front feet. The griffin was believed to be a truly extraordinary combination of the greatest of animals and the greatest of birds. Though sometimes considered evil, they were also considered noble, and were often seen on family crests.

For the first subject in the "Birds" section of *Physica*, Hildegard begins with this legendary animal. In the organization of *Physica*, Hildegard tends to begin her chapters with the more exotic animals, and then end the section with the more common. For example, this section on birds begins with the griffin, and then goes to the ostrich and the peacock, ending with the common wren.

For a healthy person, it is wholesome and healthiest for the sake of good digestion to delay the first meal until before noon or around noon. On the other hand, it is wholesome and healthy for sick, frail, and disabled people to eat breakfast in the morning in order to obtain the strength they are lacking from the food. If people desire, they may eat the same food at night, and drink the same beverage they had during the day. But people should eat in a timely manner, before nightfall, so that they can take a walk before lying down to sleep.[5]

CAUSE ET CURE (CAUSE AND CURE) 2.225–226, 10.1

☐ The Griffin

The griffin is very hot. It has some of the qualities of birds and some of the qualities of wild animals.[6] Like birds, it moves rapidly; thus, its body weight does not bring it down. Like wild animals, it eats people. When it flies in the air, it does not fly in the blazing heat, but comes near to it. Its flesh is not good for a person to eat. If people should eat its flesh, they would be greatly injured by it, since it has the qualities of a wild animal inside it. In both natures, it has defects.

When it is the time for laying its eggs, the griffin looks for a cave that is very difficult to enter, wide inside, but with a very narrow opening. Because of her fear of lions, a griffin guards her eggs carefully inside the cave. A lion can smell them from a great distance, and, if the lion finds them, will crush and break them. A griffin loathes the strength of a lion, is always on guard, and does not allow herself near one. However, she will allow a bear to approach, since a bear is weaker than a lion. She will put her eggs where neither the sun nor the wind can touch them. Neither flesh, nor eggs, nor other parts of the griffin are much use for medicine.

Since the griffin has two natures, it has more defects than perfection.

PHYSICA (BOOK OF SIMPLE MEDICINE) 6.1

~ In the Middle Ages the ostrich was a symbol of justice; the similar length of all its feathers symbolized unity. The large bird was also considered to be a creature between the birds and the beasts. In this text, Hildegard speaks about the many medicinal uses for the ostrich, a bird so hot that it cannot sit on its own eggs without cooking them! Pilgrims would return home from the East, especially Egypt, with stories about ostriches, famous for their ability to eat almost anything, including iron and stone. In Hildegard's region, most ostriches would have been living in private menageries.

☐ The Ostrich

The ostrich is very hot, since its nature is like that of animals. It has feathers like a bird but does not fly with them, since it runs very quickly, just like an animal that lives on the ground and eats from the fields. She is so hot that her eggs would burn and her chicks not hatch if she kept her eggs warm herself. For that reason she hides them in the sand, where they are warmed by the moisture and heat. After the chicks come out of the eggs, they run and follow their mother, as other birds do.

People with epilepsy should often eat the flesh of the ostrich. It will make them strong and take away the madness of the disease from them. Ostrich flesh is healthy to eat for people who are fat and vigorous, since it will diminish their superfluous flesh and make them strong. It is not good for the thin or weak, being too strong for them. Depressed people who are heavy and listless in mind should eat it often and their melancholy will lessen, making the mind pleasant and cheerful. Ostrich eggs are not good to eat, since they are poisonous. Someone who has edema should crush the eggshells from which the chicks are hatched, and put them in water. They should drink that water often, fasting or with meals, and they will be cured. The heart and lungs and other organs of the ostrich are not good for medicinal purposes, because the ostrich does not have the full strength of either birds or animals.

PHYSICA (BOOK OF SIMPLE MEDICINE) 6.2

7 In this text, Hildegard attributes insomnia to psychological factors, such as the distractions and problems mentioned here, rather than metabolic causes.

The herbs Hildegard mentions occur frequently in her remedies—fennel to make a person content; yarrow for depression; sage to diminish bad humors.

8 Hildegard experienced debilitating illnesses during her lifetime, with symptoms that resembled both migraines and depression. Though present-day sources consider her migraines to be the source of her visions, Hildegard always claimed that they came from God, rather than from a metabolic source. She does not mention her personal experience in this text.

☐ Insomnia

If it is summer time and you are distracted with some problems and cannot sleep, take fennel and twice as much yarrow.[7] Cook them briefly in
water, remove the water, put the herbs on the temples and the forehead
while still warm, and tie them with a cloth. Also, take green sage, sprin-
kle it with a little wine, and put it on the heart and around the neck. You
will be rewarded with sleep.

But if it is winter and there are no fresh herbs, take some fennel
seed and yarrow root, cook them in water, and place them on the temples and head as described. Put powdered sage, moistened with a little
wine, on the heart and around the neck, held in place with a cloth, as
described. You should have better sleep because the heat of the fennel
induces sleep, the heat of the yarrow supports sleep, and the heat of the
sage slows the heart and dilates the blood vessels in the neck, so that
sleep may continue.

CAUSE ET CURE (CAUSE AND CURE) 14; PHYSICA (BOOK OF SIMPLE MEDICINE) 1.66

☐ Migraine

Now, migraine occurs from black bile and from all the other bad humors
that are in a person.[8] It afflicts the middle of the head and not all of it,
so that sometimes it is on the right side and sometimes the left. That is,
when the humors are in excess it affects the right side, but when black
bile increases, the left. Migraine is so intense that if it affected the entire
head at one time a person could not withstand it. It is difficult to get
rid of migraines because when, on occasion, the black bile lessens, the
bad humors increase, and when the bad humors are calm, it makes the
black bile increase. This makes a cure difficult, since black bile and bad
humors are not easily calmed at the same time....

(continued on page 137)

9   This text is the preface to the section of the *Physica* devoted to an explanation of the creation and use of precious stones. Note here the interplay between the biblical stories of the fallen angels and, later on, Adam in the Garden of Eden. As usual, Hildegard's knowledge of physical science is interspersed with Scripture.

The first paragraph is filled with images of fire. Fire forms precious stones, it is a symbol of the Holy Spirit, and the Devil was defeated by fire.

A person who suffers from migraine should take dried aloe and twice the quantity of myrrh. Grind both to a very fine powder. Add wheat flour and poppy seed oil to it. Make it into a poultice. Cover the whole head, down to the ears and to the neck, place a cap over it, and leave it like this for three nights and three days. The heat of the aloe and the dryness of the myrrh, with the mildness of the wheat flour, and the coldness of the poppy seed oil, will soothe the headache. A paste made in this way supplies fattiness to the brain.

CAUSE ET CURE (CAUSE AND CURE) 14

☐ Precious Stones

All stones contain fire and moisture. The Devil hates, despises, and disdains precious stones because he remembers that their beauty appeared in him before he fell from the glory that God had given him, and also because some precious stones are created from fire, in which he received his punishments. By God's will, the Devil was defeated by fire into which he fell, just as he is defeated by the fire of the Holy Spirit whenever people are rescued from his jaws through the inspiring breath of the Holy Spirit.[9]

Precious stones and jewels originate in the East, in those areas where the heat of the sun is particularly great. From the hot sun, mountains have a great heat, like a fire. The rivers that flow in these regions always boil hot, due to the same heat of the sun. Accordingly, at times the rivers flood their banks, rising up to the mountains. The mountains, burning with the great heat of the sun, come into contact with the rivers. Foam, similar to that made by hot iron or hot stone when water is poured over it, discharges from those places where the water makes contact with the fire. The foam attaches to that place and, within three or four days, hardens into stone.

(continued on page 139)

10 After discussing the sources of precious stones and their uses, Hildegard ends the preface by explaining the connections between the first
angels and precious stones. While precious stones were briefly associated with the Devil, God allowed them to be saved so they would
bless the earth and be used as medicine. Just as Christ saved humanity
after the Fall, so God also saved precious stones to be used toward
good purposes.

Once the flood of waters has ceased and the waters have returned to the riverbed, the drops of foam dry up. They dry by the heat of the sun according to the time of the day and the temperature. Once they have dried and hardened into precious stones, they fall into the sand, like flaking fish scales. When the rivers flood again, they lift up the precious stones and deposit them in different countries, where they are eventually discovered by human beings. The mountains, where so many large stones have been found in this way, shine as bright as the light of day.

In this way, precious stones are made out of fire and water; therefore, they contain fire and moisture in them. They have many powerful qualities and effects. Many things can be done with them, but only good and honest actions, useful to human beings, not works of seduction, fornication, adultery, enmity, murder, and the like, which are vices injurious to people. For it is the nature of precious stones to seek the honest and useful effects and reject people's evil and false uses, in the same way virtues cast off vices, and vices are unable to engage with virtues.

Other kinds of stones do not originate in the mountains in the manner just described, but are produced from useless things. Using these stones, as God allows it, both good and evil can be done.

God adorned the first angel as if with precious stones. Lucifer saw them shining brightly in the mirror of divinity, and received knowledge, and realized that God wished to carry out many marvelous things. His mind was elevated with pride, because the beauty of the stones, which covered him, shone in God. He thought he could be the equal of God and more, and so his brilliance was extinguished. But, just as God raised Adam to a better part, so God allowed neither the beauty nor the virtue of those precious stones to perish, but wished them to remain in honor and blessing on earth, and used for medicine.[10]

PHYSICA (BOOK OF SIMPLE MEDICINE) 4

~ Hildegard believed that animals are a reflection of God in creation, though not as highly evolved as humans or the angels, and that many contributed to human welfare and had healing properties of their own. Though ultimately of little use for medicinal purposes, Hildegard recognizes the dog's role as a human companion, and sometimes as a protector.

11 Hildegard recognized the dog's innate ability to respond to people, and she admired their faithfulness, so much so that she believed that the Devil hated dogs the most, simply because of the love and loyalty they showed humans.

☐ The Dog

The dog is very hot and has a natural affinity for the ways of people. It knows and understands people, loves them, willingly lives with them, and is faithful to them. The Devil hates dogs because of the faithfulness they show to people.[11] When dogs recognize hatred, anger, and perfidy in a person, they often growl at them. If they know there is anger and hatred in a house, they will quietly grumble and growl. If people have treachery in them, the dog will bare his teeth at them, even though they love the dog, since it senses and understands this in people.

If thieves enter a house, the dog will snarl and growl at them. It will go after them, and stalk them and sniff at them, and in this way the thieves will be known. The dog sometimes senses in advance happy or sad events that are going to happen. According to its understanding, it sends out its voice, revealing this: When the future events are happy, it is happy and wags its tail gladly; when they are sad, it is sad and howls mournfully.

The heat in a dog's tongue confers healing on wounds and ulcers if it touches them. But if shoes are made from dog skin, it makes the feet weak and painful. It contains filth from the unclean sweat from the dog's flesh. Its flesh is of no use to humans. Indeed, its liver and innards are poisonous and its breath is harmful. If a dog bites any bread or other food, or if it imbibes from any drink, a person should not eat or drink what is left. Sometimes a dog infects these remains with poison. If people later eat or drink it, they will consume the poison themselves.

The dog has a soft and weak brain, which is sometimes touched by evil clouds. At times it smells watery and putrid vapors, in which airy spirits create their delusions and wicked whisperings. It sometimes becomes mad from this. The rest of the dog's parts are not useful for medicine.

PHYSICA (BOOK OF SIMPLE MEDICINE) 7.20

⟨∼⟩ In the Middle Ages, the unicorn was the most mentioned imaginary animal in the West. The legendary creature was never captured, but its symbolic association with virginity made it the symbol of the incarnation of God's Word, purity, and divine power. Belief in the power of the unicorn's horn and its origins persisted until the eighteenth century, when the true source of the "unicorn horn," the narwhal, a whale with an extended tooth found in the mouth of males and some females, was discovered.

12 Just as the serpent in the Garden of Eden shunned Adam and spoke to Eve, so do unicorns prefer women.

13 Hildegard was criticized for allowing only noble girls and women into her religious community. Here she argues that it is only noble girls, or virgins, who could catch the unicorn, or, by extension, serve as consecrated virgins.

☐ The Unicorn

The unicorn is more hot than cold, but its courage is greater than its heat. It eats clean plants and prances as it goes, and it flees humans and other animals, except those of its own kind, so it cannot be captured. It especially fears and shuns men; just as the serpent in the first Fall shunned the man and got to know women, so this animal turns from men and follows women.[12]

There was a certain wise man who studied the ways of animals, and he marveled greatly that this animal could not be caught by hunters of any skill. One day he went hunting, as he often did, and men, women, and girls went with him. The girls walked away from the others and played among the flowers. A unicorn, seeing the girls, stopped its prancing, sat down on its hind legs some distance from them, and gazed searchingly at them. The wise man, seeing this, thought very hard about it and realized that the unicorn could be captured by girls. Approaching the unicorn from the back, he caught it by means of those girls. For a unicorn, seeing a girl from afar, marvels that she has no beard, in spite of having the form of a person. If two or three girls are together, it is more amazed, and more readily captured while its eyes are focused on them. The girls by which unicorns are captured must be nobles, not peasants, not completely grown-up or too little, but in mid-adolescence. Those are the ones the unicorn loves because they are sweet and kind.[13]

Once a year the unicorn goes to the land that has the water of paradise. There it seeks out the finest plants and digs them up with its hooves and eats them. From them, it derives great powers, but it still flees all other animals. Beneath its horn it has something as clear as glass, so that people can look at their own face, as if in a mirror. But it is not very valuable.

Take the liver of a unicorn, grind it up, and add the powder to fat from the yolk of an egg to make an ointment. There is no form of leprosy that if smeared often with this ointment will not be cured, unless

(continued on page 145)

14 In medieval medicine, the liver of a unicorn was considered one of the few treatments for leprosy.

15 Unicorns were considered to be particularly potent in warding off evil of all kinds, including illnesses.

16 Here Hildegard suggests unicorn hoof as a means to detect poison; other medieval sources prescribe unicorn horn as an antidote for all kinds of poisons. The belief in the power of unicorns to protect against poisoning was widespread, and commonly employed in papal and royal courts.

the patient dies or God does not wish to cure the disease. The liver of this animal has good heat and is clean; the fat in the egg yolks is the most precious thing in an egg, and is just like an ointment. Leprosy is often from black bile and too much black blood.[14]

Make a belt from unicorn skin, gird yourself with it against your skin, and no strong disease or fever will harm you.[15] Make shoes from its skin and wear them, and you will always have healthy feet, legs, and hips. No diseases will harm you in these places.

People who fear being murdered by poison should put a unicorn hoof under their dinner plate, or under their drinking cup. If the food or drink is hot and poisoned, the unicorn hoof will make the food or drink boil; if the food or drink is cold, then it will smoke, and you will be able to tell there is poison there.[16] Other parts of the unicorn are not usable for medicine.

PHYSICA (BOOK OF SIMPLE MEDICINE) 4.5

Part 10
Women's Health

Although Hildegard accepted religious beliefs that supported the subordination of women, such as the injunctions of St. Paul, and she referred to herself on many occasions as a poor, frail creature, her actions reflected the belief that women are not inferior to men. Hildegard's writings on women's health support complementarity between men and women. Without women, men could not be complete; without men, women could not be complete. Hildegard believed that human beings were created as gendered, sexual beings, in body and spirit; it was through sexuality that the human spirit came into full flower. Sexual expression was a source of joy, as well as a necessity for reproduction. For Hildegard, the incarnation was the pivotal event in human history, and she asserts that the Virgin Mary, the mother of Jesus, made salvation possible. Thus, while the Fall of humanity may have come about through the sin of Eve, the salvation of humanity was made possible through Mary. Hildegard recognized the realities of sex and reproduction, and she shows a healthy knowledge of both, as well as a commitment to support women in leading whole and healthy lives. Prayer, too, is important medicine.

~ Hildegard's era was a birth-positive time; that is, successful reproduction was a priority. The medicine of the era was concerned with
enabling women to have healthy deliveries, especially given that
safe cesarean deliveries were not an option. The first example of the
operation culminating in the survival of the mother and infant was in
the year 1500, after Hildegard's time. Before then, despite rare references to the operation on living women, the primary purpose was an
attempt to retrieve the infant from a dead or dying mother; this was
done either in the hope of saving the baby's life or, more likely, so the
infant might be buried separately from its mother. The first cesarean
deliveries were always a measure of last resort, and not intended to
preserve the mother's life. Not until the nineteenth century was the
safe delivery of mother and baby through the operation possible.

Many women in Hildegard's day, rich and poor, suffered greatly and
died in childbirth, so they were encouraged to confess their sins and
receive the sacraments of the church in advance of delivery. In addition to prayer for a safe delivery, Hildegard responded to requests from
woman facing childbirth with compassion and practicality. One such
cure, as noted in *Physica* IV.10, is to keep a jasper stone on her hand
(possibly as a ring) to weaken any evil spirits that may wish to injure
the child.

1 Known as asarum in Hildegard's day, wild ginger is a genus of plants
in the birthwort family, found in Europe, North America, and Asia. The
boiled seeds and roots of fennel were used to open obstructions and
relieve pain.

2 Despite the idea that the dangers of childbirth are linked to the sin
of Eve in the Garden of Eden, Hildegard also connects women to participation in the greenness, or the vital life force that courses throughout all of creation. So important is this vital energy that in childbirth
the whole of a woman's body participates. Even the baby rejoices as it
feels the connection of its soul to this divine energy.

☐ A Difficult Birth

If a pregnant woman is suffering greatly in giving birth, carefully and with great skill boil in water and strain gentle herbs like fennel and wild ginger.[1] Squeeze out the water, and let the herbs be placed on her thighs and back, tied there gently in a linen cloth, so that her pain will be relieved and the closure of her womb will be gently opened. For the cold and harmful humors that are in women sometimes constrict and close up a pregnant woman. But if the gentle heat of the fennel and the wild ginger are strengthened in soft water over a fire, and placed around her thighs and back—since she suffers the most constriction in these areas—they will induce her womb to open.

CAUSE ET CURE (CAUSE AND CURE) 14

☐ Childbirth

When the time for birth is near, the vessel enclosing the baby is torn; the eternal greenness that took Eve from the side of Adam is present and turns upside down all corners of the cushion in the woman's body. All the foundations of the woman's body rush toward this greenness, receive it, and open up to it. They do so until the baby comes into view. Afterwards, the woman's body returns to its previous state. As the baby comes into view, its soul rejoices while it feels the eternal greenness that delivers it.[2]...

(continued on page 151)

3 The quotation is from Genesis 3:16, God's words to Eve at the expulsion from the Garden of Eden: "I will greatly multiply thy sorrow and thy conception; in sorrow thou shalt bring forth children; and thy desire shall be to thy husband, and he shall rule over thee."

4 In this last section, Hildegard notes that the recuperation time for women after childbirth varies. Certainly, in her era, while the birth of a living child was the hoped-for outcome, the possibility of fever and infections suffered by women after childbirth added to the sense of peril women experienced through childbirth.

5 In this excerpt from her discussion on conception, Hildegard explains the different conditions that contribute to the birth of either a boy or a girl infant. Some medical authorities in Hildegard's era still believed that semen was the sole source of life, and the woman's contribution was merely to incubate the child. But Hildegard agrees with those who state that children are formed and nourished from both male semen and female menstrual fluids. She also considers it generally necessary for both the man and the woman to be sexually satisfied during intercourse for conception to occur. In addition, she contends that love and affection between the couple provide the optimal conditions in the production of virtuous children.

Although Hildegard acknowledges the superiority of males in the created order, according to church doctrine, she nevertheless supports the idea that men and women are complementary as part of the divine

When children must be delivered from a woman, she is overcome by fear and trembling. Every woman trembles with this fear, and her blood vessels pour out blood in abundance, and all the joints of her body arch with tears and lamentations, as it is written: "In pain you shall bring forth children."[3]...

As the birth begins, the child comes forth with a strong flow of blood, like an overflowing stream that sweeps past stones and wood. But the bluish discharge and the offensive smell of blood cannot be purged that quickly, and thus, remain inside the mother, and are expelled little by little later on. The cleansing of a woman who is dry by nature and does not overflow with humors occurs shortly after birth. However, the cleansing of a woman who is moist by nature and abounds with humors takes longer than the cleansing of a woman who is dry and does not have many humors.[4]

CAUSE ET CURE (CAUSE AND CURE) 4, 9

☐ Conception

When a man has intercourse with a woman with an emission of strong semen, and feels love and tenderness for the woman and goes to her, and when the woman also feels tenderness for the man at the same time, a male child is conceived, since it is ordained by God. It cannot be otherwise that a male child will be conceived, since Adam, too, was formed from clay, which is stronger matter than flesh. This male child will be intelligent and virtuous, since he was conceived with strong semen and in mutual love and affection.[5]

However, if this love is lacking in the woman toward the man, but the man has tenderness and love for the woman, though the woman does not for the man, and if the semen of the man is strong, a male child will still be conceived, because the love of the man prevails. But this

(continued on page 153)

order. Although Eve is the symbol of the weaker sex because of her sin, and though she is only made out of flesh, while Adam is made of clay, men and women complete each other, and, in love, become one. In supporting a view of the need for love and affection in marriage, Hildegard offers a view of marriage that is based more on human feelings than many of her contemporaries did, a view that stresses the importance of women's satisfaction and happiness.

6 Somewhat unique for her era are Hildegard's observations of the impact of variations in female physiology and sexual behavior on the ability to bear children.

7 In some medieval texts, "flowers" is an idiomatic term for a woman's menstrual period.

8 Fertility was a major concern in Hildegard's time, when infant mortality was high and families needed children to help support the family and to inherit lands. Regular menstruation was an important indicator of fertility. According to the theory of humors, women's excess humors and waste products were cleansed by regular monthly discharges. If this did not occur, the wastes would build up and cause serious illness. Note the "greenness"—the vital life force—present in fertile women.

male child will be weak and not virtuous, since the love of the woman for the man was lacking.

If the man's seed is thin, but he feels love and tenderness toward the woman, and she has the same love for him, then a virtuous female child is created. But if the man loves the woman, but the woman does not love the man, or if the woman loves the man and he does not love her and his semen is thin at the same time, then a female child is born, due to the weakness of the semen.

But if the man's semen is strong, and neither the man nor the woman feel love for each other, a male child will be conceived because the semen was strong, but the child will be bitter due to the bitterness of his parents. If the semen is thin, and neither the man nor the woman feel love toward the other at the time, a female will be born with a bitter disposition. The heat of a woman who is obese by nature will overcome the semen of a man, so the face of the baby will often resemble her. But women who are thin by nature often produce a baby who resembles the father.[6]

CAUSE ET CURE (CAUSE AND CURE) 2.8

☐ Fertility and Infertility

For a woman, the menstrual stream shows her greenness and flowering of the blooms in her children.[7] Just as a tree, from its greenness, brings forth blossoms and leaves and bears fruit, so too woman from the greenness of the streams of menstrual blood brings forth blossoms and fruit in the womb.[8]... But young girls do not have flowing streams of menstrual blood, and therefore they do not conceive children because their bodies are not yet completed, just as there is no complete house where only the foundation has been laid and the walls not yet completed. Yet when the girl has reached the age of twelve, her body grows in strength until her fifteenth year, just as a wall is completed when it stands at its full

(continued on page 155)

9 Hildegard notes that the age of menarche, or the onset of puberty, is twelve, yet she is quick to point out that a girl is not completely mature until she reaches twenty.

10 Hildegard warns that children born to women who are not yet fully mature may not be strong.

11 In Hildegard's era, women would seek various remedies for infertility, and those who could afford it might seek many such remedies. Hildegard's letters mention such women, who came to her for her prayers, and perhaps for medical advice. In *Physica*, Hildegard recommends that infertile women eat the milt or roe of fish to enable them to conceive. In Hildegard's writings she also suggests remedies for male infertility, one of which prescribes eating fatty meat, as the text does here. Still, in the case of infertility, Hildegard always reminds those hoping to give birth that the gift of children is ultimately in God's hands.

height on the foundation. From her fifteenth until her twentieth year, the structures of her body are completed, like a house completed with beams and a roof, and into which furniture has been placed.[9] A woman who is mature in her blood vessels and in the structures of her body can easily receive and retain warm male semen. If a woman conceives a child before her twentieth year, it happens either from the extreme heat in her husband's or her own nature, or due to frequent intercourse. Nevertheless, she will produce a child that is sickly and frail.[10]...

A woman whose womb is too cold inside and too weak to conceive children can, if it is God's will, be assisted in her fertility as follows: Take the womb of a lamb or a cow that is sexually mature but still pure in that it is not and has not been pregnant. Cook it with other meat, fat, and lard, and give it to the woman to eat just before she has intercourse with her husband. She should eat such meats often. The fluid from the womb of the animals mentioned here mixes with the fluid from the woman's womb so that it becomes somewhat strengthened and built up from it and, if God wills it, she conceives much more easily. For it happens very often that, by God's judgment, the power to procreate is taken away for human beings.[11]

CAUSE ET CURE (CAUSE AND CURE) 9.1, 14

12 Lactation practices differed from one class to another in the Middle Ages, with women of the upper classes more inclined to secure the services of a wet nurse, rather than nurse their children themselves. Yet in Hildegard's era, there was no option for poor women other than to nurse their children themselves.

Hildegard agrees with a theory from Hippocrates that there is a vein connecting the uterus and the breasts. A girl's breasts were thought to keep growing until the blood vessels that lead to the uterus discharge menstruation, then they stop growing, until childbirth causes them to grow larger once again.

13 Menstruation was of significant concern to medieval medical writers and healers like Hildegard. This preoccupation with menstruation is often a characteristic of birth-positive cultures. Regular menstruation was an indication of fertility, whereas menstrual irregularities were cause for great concern. By the theory of humors, women's excess humors and buildup of bodily wastes were cleansed by regular menstruation. If this did not occur, wastes would build up in a woman's body and cause illness. Unlike some of her contemporaries, Hildegard did not believe that menstruation rendered a woman unclean, though she did believe that bloodletting rendered soldiers unclean. For Hildegard, menstruation was a natural process, not a sign of God's punishment of women, resulting from Eve's sin.

Hildegard compares menstruation to the greenness—the vital life force—that animates creation and connects all life, like the tree she mentions here.

☐ Lactation

When a woman receives semen from the man and becomes pregnant, by that natural energy the woman's blood draws upward toward her breasts. What food and drink used to turn into blood then becomes milk to feed the baby growing in its mother's womb. As the baby grows in its mother's womb, the milk increases in her breasts to nourish it.[12]

CAUSE ET CURE (CAUSE AND CURE) 4

☐ Menstruation

Just as sap begins at the root of a tree and extends upward into all of the tree's branches, so it is for women at menstruation as well. At the time of the streams of blood, the blood vessels holding her brain and supporting her vision and hearing and stimulated by this rush of blood, and the blood vessels holding the neck, back, and loins draw to themselves those of the liver, internal organs, and navel. Each blood vessel pours forth into another as a tree's sap greens its branches.[13] The blood vessels contract and release the area in which they are fastened, just as claws cut off from a small bird contract and release by means of its blood vessels.

As a gusty wind sets in motion a storm in a river, so too is a storm set in motion in all the humors in a woman's body so that they intermingle with her blood, become quite full-blooded, and are purged with this blood. This is how the stream of blood comes to pass in a woman. For that reason a woman has a headache at that time, her eyes are tired, and her entire body is fatigued. However, her eyes will not weaken if the stream comes at the right time and in the correct amount. Before the onset of this flow, those areas of her body that are supposed to receive man's semen open up so that she might conceive more easily now than at any other time. Similarly, women conceive easily at the end

(continued on page 159)

14   In this section of the text, Hildegard comments on premenstrual symptoms, such as headaches, sore eyes, and fatigue. Though other medieval medical writers consider such symptoms the price of Eve's sin in the Garden of Eden, Hildegard's approach is much less moralizing and more pragmatic and supportive.

15   Similar to her approach to premenstrual symptoms, Hildegard treats menstrual problems pragmatically, recognizing them as a medical condition, rather than a moral concern.

16   Here Hildegard compassionately writes of women who hemorrhage and/or those who experience severe menstrual pain. Her advice is for women with these symptoms to care for themselves, and for others to refrain from causing them further harm.

of menstruation, when the blood flow is diminishing, because parts of their body are constricted, like a tree that produces flowers in the summer to spread its greenness but constricts in winter.[14]...

In some younger women, because of despair, their menstrual bleeding is so seriously reduced that the vessels carrying the blood contract and dry out as a result of the woman's grief. As a tree blooms and flowers in the summer from the sun, so too are a woman's menses opened from joy, just as a cold wind, and the frost of winter, dry up the trees' leaves and branches, so too the streams of blood that flow out of a woman often dry up from melancholy. On the other hand, when due to an abundance the humors proliferate in some women and flow out, causing a contrasting and adverse suffering, then the blood vessels carrying the streams of blood constrict so that menstruation stops, because the tempests cause ill-timed coldness and excessive warmth. Thus, the blood of such women is sometimes cold, and at other times boiling hot. As a result, while their temperature changes, they run hot and cold. The blood vessels that should flow outward at a certain time are cut off, due to their aridity, and do not flow outward. There are other women who have anemic and thick tissues that grow from frailty and foulness, rather than from proper greenness. These tissues then grow over their blood vessels and suppress them so that they become seriously contracted. As a result, their streams of blood are weighed down and cannot flow outward at the correct time.[15]...

Occasionally, some women feel discomfort from various fevers and pains in the stomach, the side, and the abdomen. These pains prevent the skull from closing at the correct time, similar to the way storms cause floods when they flow over barriers. For these women, the streams of blood flow out excessively and at the wrong time. The woman then suffers as much pain as a man wounded by a sword. Consequently, medicine must be administered to her with great caution, and she should take care of herself so she will not be further harmed.[16]

CAUSE ET CURE (CAUSE AND CURE) 9.2

17 Medical authorities in the Middle Ages were certainly aware of menopause, in most cases designated as the time when women ceased menstruation and were no longer able to bear children. Medieval medical texts on the female life cycle most commonly designate the average age of menopause for women as fifty.

18 In addition to the cessation of menstruation, Hildegard points to the symptoms of dryness and irritation around bodily openings.

19 Here Hildegard notes the potential risks to babies born of older, or even younger, mothers.

20 In Hildegard's era, as now, eighty is an advanced age. Statistics indicate that before the modern era, however, if women survived their childbearing years, the possibility of their living to such an advanced age was increased, explaining the advanced ages of nuns like Hildegard. Also, while both men and women lose capacities in advanced age, Hildegard may also be pointing to increasing frailty as a sign of osteoporosis.

21 In Christian iconography the unicorn stands for Christ, who is both a miracle and a mystery of nature, to be tamed only by a virgin. The virgin is the Blessed Virgin Mary. The story of the unicorn and the virgin becomes an allegory for the incarnation of Jesus Christ.

22 In the Judeo-Christian tradition, the term *ivory tower* is a symbol of noble purity. It originates with the Song of Songs 7:4: "Thy neck is as a tower of ivory."

☐ Menopause

From her fiftieth,[17] or sometimes from her sixtieth year, a woman begins to feel irritation and dries around the openings of her body.[18]... It will be like that until her eightieth year.... From the age of fifty or, for some women, sixty, menstruation stops and the womb begins to shrink and contract so she cannot conceive children. Occasionally, however, a woman up to her eightieth year conceives a child. But this child will frequently be born with a defect, as also occurs to girls who conceive and give birth at a tender age under twenty.[19] However, from her eightieth year, a woman loses her capacity and becomes frail like the end of a day.[20]

CAUSE ET CURE (CAUSE AND CURE) 9.2

☐ When the Virgin Captured the Unicorn

It came to pass when the Virgin captured the unicorn[21] and when God saw that it was right, God made the pure and virginal ivory tower.[22] In this work, God's plan was perfected, that is, because God became human. Because it was the woman who obeyed the word of the serpent and cast the entire world into darkness, so death entered into her and she became a weak creature. Every creature that was once strong and noble became debilitated because of her vulnerability. Yet God destined in her a great plan so miraculous that neither the angels nor humankind nor any creature can fully understand it. In God's ancient design a virgin in the sunlight reversed the fall of woman, transforming it into

(continued on page 163)

23   In the Middle Ages, one of the names for Mary was the "light of God" and she was depicted bathed in a brilliant light.

24   This text is an excerpt from a sermon Hildegard gave at her former monastery of Disibodenberg in 1171, preserved in the form of a letter to the abbot. The fact that she presented the sermon to the monks there is noted within the letter itself. Abbot Helengerus was the successor of Juno, the abbot at the time when Hildegard and her nuns left Disibodenberg. Correspondence indicates that Helengerus had his shortcomings, and Hildegard did not refrain from writing to him harshly on occasion, though he also tried to make peace between Disibodenberg and Rupertsberg. This sermon focuses on Hildegard's explanation of the workings of God in all creation and through salvation history. Although this text is not about women's health, per se, it does explain Hildegard's views about the crucial role of women in salvation history.

Here Hildegard reveals her predominantly positive vision of womanhood. Like other early and medieval theological authors, she ties all women to Eve, who ate the fruit of the Tree of Knowledge of Good and Evil in the Garden of Eden, and, thereafter, humanity was fallen. But Hildegard ends the story with a twist. That is, though all women are connected to Eve, they are also all connected to the Virgin Mary. A woman may have brought sin into the world, but it was also through a woman that God chose to become human, and thereby reverse the Fall. Of course, this was all very confusing to the Devil, who tricked the woman in the Garden of Eden, but God eventually bettered him through the Virgin Mary, totally unexpectedly!

good.[23] God did this to confuse the Devil who had tricked the woman; he was completely unaware of what was to be accomplished through her in much the same way as he did not understand God. Thus, he was deprived of all joy and buried in hell.[24]

TO ABBOT HELENGERUS OF DISIBODENBERG, CA. 1171; *EPISTOLARIUM* (LETTERS) 77R

Part 11
Worldly Witness

Hildegard's influence extended far beyond her own monastery, and beyond the religious community. In addition to her prophetic role in the church, she was an advocate for justice and compassion in worldly affairs. Her correspondents included secular rulers, local nobles, and foreign royalty who sought her advice and "worldly witness." Hildegard would address them sternly when she felt they deserved it. She deeply believed that the political and social power of the elite was a privilege that brought with it responsibility for others and the need to set a good moral example. Concerned with the alleviation of human suffering, Hildegard challenged those with political power to be fair and just rulers. Immersed in the political events of her day, and knowledgeable about the dangers faced by people in the world, she offered her correspondents advice, comfort, and challenge.

1 Eleanor (1122–1203) was duchess of Aquitaine and countess of Poitou and actively governed in her own right. She was queen of France as the wife of Louis VII, duchess of Normandy, countess of Anjou, and queen of England as the wife of Henry Plantagenet. While she did not rule her lands independent of her husbands, she served as regent for both husbands and sons. Through her own marriages and those of her children, Eleanor was related to many of the ruling houses of Europe. An active patron of the arts, Eleanor was one of the most renowned women of her era. Unfortunately, this small fragment of a letter is the only evidence we have of a correspondence between Hildegard and Eleanor. However, the fact that they were in contact at all is notable. Hildegard offers Eleanor spiritual and emotional support; her advice to Eleanor's husband, Henry, king of England, was stronger, warning him against following his own will instead of justice. (See Hildegard's letter to Henry, which follows.)

Though we do not know the exact context of this letter, it is clear that Hildegard is urging Eleanor to keep a cool head and to trust that God will support her in her tribulations. Her marriage to Henry flourished in the early years, when she served as regent, gave birth to their children, and gained political control of the Aquitaine in 1168. However, later their relationship was stormy, particularly after her participation in her son's revolt against their father, the king. That led to her imprisonment 1174, which did not end until Henry's death in 1189. These events may have contributed to the tribulations mentioned by Hildegard.

2 Henry II (1133–1189) ruled England for thirty-five years and was the husband of the famous Eleanor of Aquitaine. This brief letter is one example of Hildegard's correspondence with secular rulers. Scholars believe the letter was written before 1170, when followers of Henry murdered the archbishop of Canterbury, Thomas Becket, in the cathedral. Becket was canonized by Pope Alexander III shortly after his death.

☐ Advice to Eleanor of Aquitaine

Your mind is like a wall covered in clouds, and you look all around, but have no rest. Stay calm, stand firm, and find stability in God and your fellow creatures, and God will help you in all your tribulations. May God give you his blessing and help in all your works.[1]

To Eleanor of Aquitaine, Queen of England, ca. 1154–1170;
Epistolarium (Letters) 318

☐ The Duty of a King

To a certain man who holds a certain office, the Lord says: "Yours are the gifts of giving: It is by ruling and defending, protecting and providing, that you may reach heaven." But a black bird comes to you from the north, and says: "You can do whatever you want; so do this and do that; make this excuse and that excuse, for it does not profit you to have regard to justice; for if you always look for her, you are not the master but the slave." Do not listen to the thief that is advising you like this, for he is the one who stripped you of great glory, when from dust you were created, a beautiful form from ashes, and received the vital spark of life. Look more intently to the Father who created you, because your mind is well-intentioned, and you willingly do good unless you are influenced by the squalid habits of those around you, as you have been for a time.

(continued on page 163)

In the body of the letter, Hildegard urges Henry to be a good king and to rule justly. His chief liability, according to Hildegard, is his tendency to take advice from the wrong people. The letter urges him to stop listening to those with weak morals and seek guidance from God instead. God will be there for him, she advises.

3   Frederick Barbarossa (1122–1190) succeeded his uncle, King Conrad III, as Holy Roman emperor in 1152. He is considered by many historians to be one of the greatest medieval emperors. Upon his accession, he had several goals in mind, namely, to end the civil unrest of the last seventy-five years, to reinvigorate the Holy Roman Empire, and, notably, to subjugate the papacy under his power. At the beginning of his reign there was great optimism, and Hildegard took the opportunity to write to welcome him shortly after he became king. She was even invited to court in Ingelheim for a visit. But Hildegard was not happy with Frederick's actions in regard to the papacy, and it strained their relationship. In 1153, Frederick deposed Archbishop Heinrich of Mainz, one of Hildegard's closest allies. However, ten years later he proclaimed her abbess of St. Rupertsberg outright, which was to Hildegard's advantage.

It is likely that this letter was written during a time when Frederick gave his support to his second antipope. Hildegard rebukes him, cautioning that his lack of skill in governance may lead him to lose God's grace. Eminent Hildegard scholar Bruce Hozeski commented on her savvy in regard to political situations involving church and state: "Hildegard's clear intelligence foresaw that the abuse in the political situation, the corrupt government of the episcopal electors and the princely abbots, was exasperating to the Germans and that the volatile situation would eventually burst into flames in some event such as the eventual Reformation or the Thirty Years' War" (*Hildegard of Bingen's Mystical Visions,* trans. Bruce Hozeski [Rochester, VT: Bear & Company, 1983], xxx).

Dear son of God, flee from these things, and call on your Father, for he gladly reaches out his hand to help you.[2]

Now, may you live forever, and dwell in eternal felicity.

TO HENRY II OF ENGLAND, CA. 1154–1170; EPISTOLARIUM (LETTERS) 317

☐ Political Advice for the Emperor

O king, it is important for you to undertake all your affairs with caution. For in a mystic vision I see you as a little boy or some madman before the Living Eyes. You have some time yet for ruling over earthly matters. However, beware that the almighty King does not lay you low because of the blindness of your eyes, because you do not see how to correctly hold the rod of governance. See to it that your actions do not cause you to lose the grace of God![3]

TO EMPEROR FREDERICK BARBAROSSA, 1164; EPISTOLARIUM (LETTERS) 313

⟿ This text is from a letter to Philip of Alsace (1143–1191), count of Flanders from 1168 to 1191. He went on his first crusade in 1177. In this letter Hildegard cautions Philip to live under God's law and justice.

4   Hildegard warns Philip about the use of unjust violence, and of his responsibility as a commander to control those in his armies who dare to kill unjustly. She reminds him that God would rather give the unconverted an opportunity to change than to have them die as sinners. Given her era, this was a relatively compassionate response to those who were not Christian.

5   However, Hildegard reasons, if there is no other option, and the godless seem bent on destruction, then by all means act in self-defense, and God's grace will go with you.

6   This brief letter is to a laywoman regarding her husband's health, and is an example of Hildegard's stature, as well as the people from many walks of life who sought her help. Hildegard had an influence on local laypeople, and Luitgard may also have had a family connection to Rupertsberg. In this letter Hildegard warns Luitgard that her husband is not likely to recover; thus, she should see to her affairs and warn him about the state of his soul.

☐ A Warning about the Use of Violence

So, son of God, be careful to look with the pure eye of justice, just as the eagle does on the sun, and you will make good decisions, untainted by selfishness. Otherwise, the Judge of all, who gave his command to humankind, whom he calls to himself through penitence, may ask you: "Why did you go and kill your neighbor without my justice?" You also should constrain those people who would commit homicide, under judgment of the law and fear of death in accordance with the writings of the pillars of the church. You must contemplate the things you have ignored, such as your sins and your unjust decisions. Make the sign of the cross and come back to the living God who is the way and the truth, who does not desire the death of sinners, but that they turn from the wrong way and live.[4]

However, if the time comes that the godless wish to destroy the fountain of faith, then resist them as best you can, through the grace of God.[5]

To Philip I, Count of Flanders, ca. 1175–1177; *Epistolarium* (Letters) 324

☐ To a Wife on Her Husband's Health

O Creature of God, Luitgard, arrange your affairs according to your needs, because I do not see your husband's health returning before his end. Therefore, beseech, correct, and warn him for the safety of his soul, as I see much darkness in him. May God look upon you, that you may live forever.[6]

To Luitgard of Karlsberg, before 1170; *Epistolarium* (Letters) 336

~ This text is from a letter to Countess Oda of Eberstein. The counts of Eberstein were a noble family in southwest Germany. From 1085 until the thirteenth century, they lived in the castle known today as Alt Eberstein. This text is an excerpt from a longer letter in which Hildegard gives advice to a noblewoman. From Hildegard's existing correspondence, it appears that many such women wrote Hildegard, asking for advice, prayers, encouragement, and the like. This letter is an interesting example of Hildegard's belief in the role of the nobility to use their position for the good of others. Though she was of the noble class, and associated mostly with her noble counterparts, Hildegard had a strong belief that the privileged are entrusted by God with their position to be generous and merciful to other people. In a world where many people exploited their wealth and social position for personal gain, Hildegard held them to a high moral standard, and, because of her own background, she was in a position to make the challenge. In this case, Hildegard is compassionate but also impatient with Oda's propensity to vacillate between secular pursuits and good works.

7 Though Hildegard clearly believes the monastic life is the highest vocation, she is not inclined to let those in the secular world forget that God is calling them, too, to a vocation as married people in the world.

☐ The Role of Nobility

You pray, saying: "My guilt is too great in the wound of my sins." But later on you wither in the streets—that is, in your self-will—and you rush to secular pursuits, rather than doing good works and exercising your moral muscles. The longing in your heart says: "I wish to do good works." But these thoughts never come to fruition, so that you wither in your sins. Therefore, cry out through good works and God will sustain you.

Listen! Pay attention that you wither up evil things, and grow greenness in good. Cry out and begin to see God in goodwill, and perfect yourself in good works. The person who does good works sees God, but the person who only thinks about good works is like a mirror where the image is reflected, but not really there. Rise up again and begin good works and bring them to perfection and God will sustain you. But, you will say: "I have a husband, and I am of the secular world. What is this that you are calling me to do?"[7] I say in response that you should have mercy, charity, and virtue—which trample pride underfoot. Also, you should give a helping hand to the weak and those debilitated by their troubles; be merciful to those who sin against you, so that you do not engage in idol worship, which is greed; and, you should not slap God in the face, that is, resent the happiness of another, or you will fall into envy. Then you will live.

TO COUNTESS ODA OF EBERSTEIN, CA. 1153–1154; *EPISTOLARIUM* (LETTERS) 326

⟨∿⟩   Bertha of Sulzbach (ca. 1110–1159) was the first wife and empress of Byzantine emperor Manuel I Comnenus; after her marriage in 1146, she was known as Empress Irene. She was renowned for her piety and modesty. An archbishop accused of heresy reportedly put a curse on her womb so she could not bear sons. Irene and her husband had two daughters.

8   In this lovely section, Hildegard reminds Irene that God is present in the world around us, showering us with love and abundance, and cleansing us. Those of us who are happy in God will not be endangered by loud blasts from unsavory characters, perhaps even archbishops who put curses on us!

9   Hildegard is characteristically careful here, and does not state that God will bring Irene the child she wants. But Hildegard does assure the empress that she prays for her, and that God is with her.

☐ To Empress Irene on Her Desire for a Child

The breath of the spirit of God speaks: In wintertime, God covers the branch in love. In summertime, God brings forth greenness and an abundance of flowers, removing disease that may cause the branch to wither. It is through the springs out of the rock in the East that other waters are cleansed, and run more swiftly, having no dirt in them. These lessons apply to every person whom God grants one day of happiness and the glowing sunrise of honor. Such people will not be oppressed by the strong north wind, with its foul blast from hostile characters.[8]

Look to the God who has moved you and who seeks burnt offerings from your heart. Sigh for the Divine. May God grant you the joy of the child you want. The living eye of God looks upon you, and desires you, and you will live for all eternity.[9]

TO EMPRESS IRENE, CA. 1146–1159; *EPISTOLARIUM* (LETTERS) 319

The Works of Hildegard of Bingen ☐

The Visionary Trilogy

Liber scivias domini (Know the Ways of the Lord; often simply called *Scivias*), 1141–1151

Liber vitae meritorum (Book of Life's Merits), 1158–1163

Liber divinorum operum (Book of the Divine Works), 1163–1174

Natural Science

Liber subtilitatum diversarum naturum creaturam (Book on the Subtleties of Many Kinds of Creatures), 1151–1158, which includes *Physica* (Physical Things; also known as *Liber simplices medicinae*, Book of Simple Medicine) and *Cause et cure* (Cause and Cure; also known as *Liber compositae medicinae*, Book of Compound Medicine)

Morality Play

Ordo Virtutum (Play of the Virtues), 1150s

Miscellaneous Works

Epistolarium (Letters), ca. 1147–1179

Expositiones Evangeliorum (Homilies on the Gospels), 1160s–1170s

Litterae ignotae (Unknown Writings), 1150s

Lingua ignota (Unknown Language), 1150s

Explanatio Regulae Sancti Benedictini (Explanation of the Rule of St. Benedict), 1150s–early 1160s

Vita Sancti Ruperti (Life of St. Rupert), possibly 1150s, or 1170–1173

Explanatio Symboli Sancti Athanasii (Explanation of the Athanation Creed), ca. 1170

Vita Sancti Disibodi (Life of St. Disibod), 1170

Solutiones triginta octo questionum (Solutions to Thirty-Eight Questions), 1176

Songs

Symphonia armonie celestium revelationum (Symphony of the Harmony of Celestial Revelations), 1150s

A Note on Sources ☐

I would like to thank the staff of the Claremont School of Theology Library, who provided me exemplary support in obtaining the necessary sources for this project. Fortunately, the Wiesbaden Codex is available online. Two nineteenth-century sources were especially useful: *Analecta Sanctae Hildegardis*, in *Analecta Sacra*, vol. 8, edited by Jean-Baptiste Pitra (Monte Cassino, Italy: Typis Sacri Montis Casinensis, 1882), and *Patrologia Latina*, vol. 197 (Turnhout, Belgium: Brepols, 1855), also available online. The following critical editions from the Corpus Christianorum Continuatio Mediaevalis were instrumental in providing many of Hildegard's original works in Latin:

> *Epistolarium pars prima I-XC*, edited by L. Van Acker, Corpus Christianorum Continuatio Mediaevalis CCCM 91A (Turnhout, Belgium: Brepols, 1991).

> *Epistolarium pars secunda XCI-CCLr*, edited by L. Van Acker, Corpus Christianorum Continuatio Mediaevalis CCCM 91A (Turnhout, Belgium: Brepols, 1993).

> *Epistolarium pars tertia CCLI-CCCXC*, edited by L. Van Acker and M. Klaes-Hachmoller, Corpus Christianorum Continuatio Mediaevalis XCIB (Turnhout, Belgium: Brepols, 2001).

> *Liber divinorum operum*, edited by A. Derolez and P. Dronke, Corpus Christianorum Continuatio Mediaevalis CCCM 92 (Turnhout, Belgium: Brepols, 1996).

> *Liber vitae meritorum*, edited by A. Carlevaris, Corpus Christianorum Continuatio Mediaevalis CCCM 90 (Turnhout, Belgium: Brepols, 1995).

> *Opera minora*, edited by H. Feiss, C. Evans, B. M. Kienzle, C. Muessig, B. Newman, and P. Dronke, Corpus Christianorum Continuatio Mediaevalis CCCM 226 (Turnhout, Belgium: Brepols, 2007).

> *Opera minora* II, edited by C. P. Evans, J. Deploige, S. Moens, M. Embach, and K. Gärtner, Corpus Christianorum Continuatio Mediaevalis CCCM 226 (Turnhout, Belgium: Brepols, 2014).

Scivias, edited by A. Führkötter and A. Carlevaris, Corpus Christianorum Scholars Version vols. 43 and 43A (Turnhout, Belgium: Brepols,
2003).

Vitae Sanctae Hildegardis, edited by M. Klaes, Corpus Christianorum Continuatio Mediaevalis CCM 126 (Turnhout, Belgium: Brepols,
1993).

In addition, the following critical editions were helpful in the completion
of this book:

Cause et cure, edited by Paul Kaiser (Basel, Switzerland: Hildegard-
Gesellschaft, 1980).

Cause et cure, edited by L. Moulinier (Berlin: Akademie Verlag, 2003).

Marianne Richert Pfau and Stefan J. Morent, *Hildegard von Bingen: Der Klang des Himmels (Europäische Komponistinnen, Band 1)*
(Cologne, Germany: Boehlau Verlag, 2005).

*Symphonia: A Critical Edition of the Symphonia Armonie Celestium
Revelationum* (Symphony of the Harmony of Celestial Revelations),
with introduction, translations, and commentary by Barbara Newman (Ithaca, NY: Cornell University Press, 1988).*

Symphonia: Gedichte und Gesänge—Lateinisch und Deutsch, edited
by Walter Berschin and Heinrich Schipperges (Gerlingen, Germany:
Lambert Schneider, 1995).

*Two Hagiographies: Vita Sancti Rupperti Confessoris, Vita Sancti
Dysibodi Episcopi*, edited and translated by Hugh Feiss and Christo-
pher P. Evans, Dallas Medieval Texts and Translations 11 (Leuven and
Paris: Peeters, 2010).

---

* The numbering of the songs in this book follows the order set by Barbara Newman in her
critical edition, *Symphonia* (Ithaca, NY: Cornell University Press, 1998). For a full list of the
songs in *Symphonia* see the International Society of Hildegard of Bingen Studies: Music,
www.hildegard-society.org/p/music.html.

Notes

1. Gottfried of Disibodenberg and Theodoric of Echternach, *The Life of Saintly Hildegard*, trans. Hugh Feiss, OSB (Toronto: Peregrine Publishing, 1996), 44.

2. Beverly Mayne Kienzle, Jenny Bledsoe, and Stephen H. Belnke, *Hildegard of Bingen: Solutions to Thirty-Eight Questions* (Athens, OH: Cistercian Publications, 2014), 2.

3. Gottfried of Disibodenberg and Theodoric of Echternach, *The Life of Saintly Hildegard*, 15.

4. Hildegard Ryan, OSB, "St. Hildegard of Bingen (1098–1179) and Jutta of Sponheim (1084–1136)," in *Medieval Women Monastics: Wisdom's Wellsprings*, edited by Miriam Schmitt, OSM, and Linda Kulzer, OSB (Collegeville, MN: Liturgical Press, 1996), 150–151.

5. Claudia Nolte, "Hildegard of Bingen and Ramon Lull: Two Approaches to Medieval Spirituality," *Magistra* (January 1, 2000): 220–221.

6. Barbara Newman, *Sister of Wisdom: St. Hildegard's Theology of the Feminine* (Berkeley: University of California Press, 1987), 23.

7. Julie Hotchin, "Enclosure and Containment: Jutta and Hildegard at the Abbey of St. Disibod," *Magistra* (January 1, 1996): 132.

8. Jo Ann McNamara, "Forward to the Past: Hildegard of Bingen and Twelfth-Century Monastic Reform," in *Explanation of the Rule of Benedict by Hildegard of Bingen*, trans. Hugh Feiss, OSB (Eugene, OR: Wipf and Stock, 2005), 12–15.

9. Kevin Madigan, *Medieval Christianity: A New History* (New Haven, CT: Yale University Press, 2015), 119–150.

10. McNamara, "Forward to the Past," 16–18.

11. Bernard McGuinn and Patricia Ferris McGuinn, *Early Christian Mystics: The Divine Vision of the Spiritual Masters* (New York: Crossroads, 2003), 100.

12. Barbara Newman, *Voice of the Living Light: Hildegard and Her World* (Berkeley: University of California Press, 1998), 1.

13. McNamara, "Forward to the Past," 18–20.

14. Feiss, trans., *Explanation of the Rule of Benedict by Hildegard of Bingen*, 5.

15. "Hildegard von Bingen/The Monastery," www.landderhildegard.de /her-life/work-as-abbess/foundation-of-the-monastery (accessed July 29, 2015).

16. McNamara, "Forward to the Past," 34.

17. Gottfried of Disibodenberg and Theodoric of Echternach, *The Life of Saintly Hildegard*, 16.

18. McNamara, "Forward to the Past," 20; see also 34.

19. Beverly Mayne Kienzle and Pamela J. Walker, *Women Preachers and Prophets through Two Millennia of Christianity* (Berkeley: University of California Press, 1998), 143.
20. Ryan, "St. Hildegard of Bingen (1098–1179) and Bl. Jutta of Sponheim (1084–1136): Foremothers of Wisdom," 151.
21. Gottfried of Disibodenberg and Theodoric of Echternach, *The Life of Saintly Hildegard*, 60.
22. McGuinn and McGuinn, *Early Christian Mystics*, 100–103.
23. Ibid.
24. Charles Burnett and Peter Dronke, eds., *Hildegard of Bingen: The Context of Her Thought and Art* (London: Warburg Institute, 1998), 198–199.
25. Oliver Sacks, *The Man Who Mistook His Wife for a Hat and Other Clinical Tales* (New York: Simon & Schuster, 1998), 168.
26. *Hildegard of Bingen: Scivias*, trans. Mother Columba Hart and Jane Bishop (Mahwah, NJ: Paulist Press, 1990), 60.
27. Avis Clendenen, "Hildegard, Jung and the Dark Side of God," *Magistra* (December 1, 2010): 105.
28. Gottfried of Disibodenberg and Theodoric of Echternach, *The Life of Saintly Hildegard*, 51.
29. Ibid.
30. Ibid.
31. Ibid.
32. "Bingen, Hildegard of 1098–1179," *Encyclopedia of Sex and Gender: Culture Society History*, ed. Fedwa Malti-Douglas (Farmington Hills, MI: Thomson Gale / Macmillan Reference 2007), 193–196.
33. Gottfried of Disibodenberg and Theodoric of Echternach, *The Life of Saintly Hildegard*, 52.
34. Ibid.
35. Gerda Lerner, *The Creation of Feminist Consciousness: From Middle Ages to 1870* (New York: Oxford University Press, 1993), 52.
36. Kienzle and Walker, *Women Preachers and Prophets*, 137.
37. Newman, *Voice of the Living Light*, 1.
38. Kienzle and Walker, *Women Preachers and Prophets*, 147.
39. Ryan, "Foremothers of Wisdom," 159; Peter Dronke, *Women Writers of the Middle Ages* (New York: Cambridge University Press, 1984), 196.
40. Letter to Archbishop Christian of Mainz, 1179, *Epistolarium* (Letters) 24.
41. Anna Silvas, OSB, trans., "Saint Hildegard of Bingen: *The Vita Sanctae Hildegardis*," *Tjurunga* 29 (1985); *Tjurunga* 32 (1987): 57–58.
42. Newman, *Voice of the Living Light*, 1.
43. "Bingen, Hildegard of 1098–1179," *Encyclopedia of Sex and Gender*, 230.

44. Madigan, *Medieval Christianity*, 419.
45. Diane K. Hawkins, "Hildegard von Bingen, 1098–1179: German Medical Author, Composer, and Visionary Mystic," *Science and Its Times* (January 1, 2001): 191.
46. Victoria Sweet, *God's Hotel: A Doctor, a Hospital, and a Pilgrimage to the Heart of Medicine* (New York: Penguin Books, 2012), 200–204.
47. "The Life and Works of Hildegard von Bingen (1098–1179)," *Internet History Sourcebook Project*, www.fordham.edu/halsall/med/hildegarde.asp (accessed January 14, 2013); Margot Fassler, *Music in the Medieval West: Western Music in Context* (New York: W. W. Norton, 2014), 141.
48. Kienzle et al., *Hildegard of Bingen*, 4.
49. Ibid., 1.
50. Ibid., 13.
51. Carl McColman, *Answering the Contemplative Call* (Newburyport, MA: Hampton Roads, 2013), 16–19.
52. Patricia Ranft, *A Women's Way: The Forgotten History of Women Spiritual Directors* (New York: Palgrave, 2000), 79.
53. Fassler, *Music in the Medieval West*, 137–138.
54. Ryan, "Foremothers of Wisdom," 156.
55. Olivia Carter Mather, "The Music of Hildegard von Bingen," http://the-orb.net/encyclop/culture/music/mather.htm (accessed July 21, 2015). See https://web.archive.org/web/20150415063858/http://the-orb.net/encyclop/culture/music/mather.htm.
56. "Hildegard of Bingen: Symphony of the Harmony of Heaven"; http://hildegard.org/music/music.html (accessed July 29, 2015).
57. Grove Music Online, "Hildegard of Bingen," www.mifami.org/eLibrary/Hildegard_of_Bingen-Grove_Music-Article.htm (accessed May 27, 2013).
58. Mather, "The Music of St. Hildegard," 4–9.
59. Grove Music Online, "Hildegard of Bingen."
60. Anne H. King-Lenzmeier, *Hildegard of Bingen: An Integrated Vision* (Collegeville, MN: Liturgical Press, 2011), 120.
61. "Hildegard of Bingen: Symphony of the Harmony of Heaven."
62. Judy Keane, "Why Gregorian Chant Rocks," http://catholicexchange.com/why-gregorian-chant-rocks (accessed July 27, 2015).
63. Ibid.
64. "Hildegard of Bingen: Symphony of the Harmony of Heaven."
65. Ibid.
66. Ibid.

Suggested Resources ☐

Books about Hildegard

Clendenen, Avis. *Experiencing Hildegard: Jungian Perspectives,* rev. ed. Wilmette, IL: Chiron, 2012.

Dreyer, Elizabeth A. *Holy Power, Holy Presence: Rediscovering Medieval Metaphors for the Holy Spirit.* Mahwah, NJ: Paulist Press, 2007.

Fox, Matthew. *Illuminations of Hildegard of Bingen.* Rochester, VT: Inner Traditions, 1985.

Kienzle, Beverly Mayne, Debra L. Stoudt, and George Ferzoco. *A Companion to Hildegard of Bingen.* Boston: Brill, 2013.

Kienzle, Beverly Mayne, and Pamela J. Walker. *Women Preachers and Prophets through Two Millennia of Christianity.* Berkeley: University of California, 1998.

King-Lenzmeier, Anne H. *Hildegard of Bingen: An Integrated Vision.* Collegeville, MN: Liturgical Press, 2001.

Ryan, Hildegard. "St. Hildegard of Bingen (1098–1179) and Bl. Jutta of Sponheim (1084–1136): Foremothers of Wisdom." In *Medieval Women Monastics: Wisdom's Wellsprings*, edited by Miriam Schmitt, OSB, and Linda Kulzer, OSB. Collegeville, MN: Liturgical Press, 1996.

Schipperges, Heinrich. *Hildegard of Bingen: Healing and the Nature of the Cosmos.* Princeton, NJ: Markus Wiener, 1998.

Strehlow, Wighard. *Hildegard of Bingen's Spiritual Remedies.* Rochester, VT: Healing Arts Press, 2002.

Translations of Hildegard's Works

Atherton, Mark, trans. *Hildegard of Bingen: Selected Writings.* New York: Penguin Books, 2001.

Baird, Joseph L., ed. *The Personal Correspondence of Hildegard of Bingen.* New York: Oxford University Press, 2006.

Baird, Joseph L., and Radd K. Ehrmann, trans. *The Letters of Hildegard of Bingen.* 3 vols. New York: Oxford University Press, 1994–2004.

Berger, Margaret, trans. *Hildegard of Bingen, On Natural Philosophy and Medicine: Selections from Cause et cure.* Suffolk, UK: D. S. Brewer, 1999.

Butcher, Carmen Acevedo. *Hildegard of Bingen, Doctor of the Church: A Spiritual Reader.* Brewster, MA: Paraclete Press, 2013.

Dronke, Peter, ed. *Nine Medieval Latin Plays.* Cambridge, NY: Cambridge University Press 1994.

———. *Women Writers of the Middle Ages: A Critical Study of Texts from Perpetua to Marguerite Porete*. Cambridge, NY: Cambridge University Press, 1984.

Fox, Matthew, ed. *Hildegard of Bingen's Book of Divine Works: With Letters and Songs*. Rochester, VT: Inner Traditions, 1987.

Gottfried of Disibodenberg and Theodoric of Echternach. *The Life of the Saintly Hildegard*. Translated by Hugh Feiss. Toronto: Peregrine Publishing, 1996.

Hart, Mother Columba, trans. *Hildegard of Bingen: Scivias*. Classics of Western Spirituality. Mahwah, NJ: Paulist Press, 1990.

Higley, Sarah L. *Hildegard of Bingen's Unknown Language: An Edition, Translation, and Discussion*. New York: Palgrave Macmillan, 2007.

Hildegard of Bingen. *Explanation of the Rule of Benedict*. Translated by Hugh Feiss. Eugene, OR: Wipf & Stock, 2005.

Hozeski, Bruce, trans. *The Book of the Rewards of Life: Liber Vitae Meritorum*. New York: Oxford University Press, 1997.

———. *Hildegard's Healing Plants: From Her Medieval Classic Physica*. Boston: Beacon Press, 2002.

———. *Hildegard of Bingen's Mystical Visions: Translated from Scivas*. Santa Fe, NM: Bear, 1995.

Kienzle, Beverly Mayne. *Hildegard of Bingen and Her Gospel Homilies: Speaking New Mysteries*. Turnhout, Belgium: Brepols, 2009.

———, trans. *Hildegard of Bingen: Homilies on the Gospels*. Collegeville, MN: Cistercian, 2011.

Kienzle, Beverly Mayne, Jenny C. Bledsoe, and Stephen H. Behnke, trans. *Hildegard of Bingen: Solutions to Thirty-Eight Questions*. Collegeville, MN: Cistercian, 2014.

Newman, Barbara. *Sister of Wisdom: St. Hildegard's Theology of the Feminine*. Berkeley: University of California Press, 1997.

———, trans. *Symphonia: A Critical Edition of the "Symphonia armonie celestium Revelationum."* 2nd ed. Ithaca, NY: Cornell University Press, 1998.

———, ed. *Voice of the Living Light: Hildegard of Bingen and Her World*. Berkeley: University of California Press, 1998.

Throop, Priscilla, trans. *Hildegard von Bingen's Physica*. Rochester, VT: Inner Traditions, 1998.

Discography

Anima. *Circle of Wisdom: Songs of Hildegard von Bingen*. Anima, 1998.

———. *Sacred Music of the Middle Ages: Hildegard of Bingen (1098–1179) and Others*. DRT Productions, 1994.

Anonymous 4. *11,000 Virgins: Chants for the Feast of Saint Ursula*. Harmonia Mundi, 1997.

———. *The Origin of Fire: Music and Visions of Hildegard von Bingen*. Harmonia Mundi, 2005.

Braslavsky, Catherine. *Marriage of the Heavens and the Earth*. Jade Records, 2008.

Early Music Institute. *The Lauds of Saint Ursula*. Focus 911, 1991.

Gentile, Norma. *Healing Chants by Hildegard of Bingen*. Vol 1. Healing Chants Media, 2002.

Gothic Voices. *A Feather on the Breath of God: Sequences and Hymns by Abbess Hildegard of Bingen*. Hyperion, 1993.

The Hildegard Singers. *O Greenest Branch: Songs of St. Hildegard of Bingen*. The Hildegard Singers, 2015.

Jouissance. *Viriditas*. Spectrum/Cistercian, 1993.

The Lady Chapel Singers. *Echoes of St. Hildegard*. Church Publishing, 2003.

———. *Meditation Chants of Hildegard von Bingen*. Healing Chants Media, 2009.

———. *Unfurling Love's Creation: Chants by Hildegard von Bingen*. Healing Chants Media, 2015.

Oak, Ellen. *The Harmony of Heaven*. Bison Publications, 1995.

Sequentia. *900 Years*. 8 compact discs. Deutsche Harmonia Mundi, 1998.

———. *Canticles of Ecstasy*. Deutsche Harmonia Mundi, 2010.

———. *Celestial Hierarchy*. Deutsche Harmonia Mundi, 2013.

———. *Music for Paradise: The Best of Hildegard von Bingen*. Sony Masterworks, 2012.

———. *O Jerusalem*. Deutsche Harmonia Mundi, 1997.

———. *Ordo virtutum*. 2 compact discs. Deutsche Harmonia Mundi, 1998.

———. *Saints*. 2 compact discs. Deutsche Harmonia Mundi, 1998.

———. *Sequentia: Hildegard von Bingen*. 8 compact discs. Sony Music, 2014.

———. *Symphoniae: Geistliche Gesänge* (Spiritual Songs). Deutsche Harmonia Mundi, 1993.

———. *Visions of Paradise: A Hildegard von Bingen Anthology*. Deutsche Harmonia Mundi/Sony Classical, 2009.

———. *Voice of the Blood*. Deutsche Harmonia Mundi/BMG Classics, 1995.

Sinfonye. *Aurora: The Complete Hildegard von Bingen*. Vol 2. Celestial Harmonies, 1997.

———. *Hildegard*. Decca Classics, 2012.

————. *O nobilissima viriditas: The Complete Hildegard von Bingen*. Vol. 3. Celestial Harmonies, 2004.

————. *Symphony of the Harmony of Celestial Revelations*. Vol. 1. Celestial Harmonies, 1996.

Souther, Richard. *Illumination (Hildegard of Bingen: The Fires of the Spirit)*. Sony Classical, 1997.

————. *Vision: The Music of Hildegard von Bingen*. Angel Records, 1994.

Film

Hildegard. With Patricia Routledge. Directed by Roger Thomas. Worcester, PA: Vision Video, 2006.

Hildegard of Bingen and the Living Light. Written and performed by Linn Maxwell. Directed by Erv Raible. Alto, MI: Alto Productions, 2012.

Hildegard of Bingen in Portrait: Ordo Virtutum, Vox Animae. 2 discs. London: Opus Arte, 2003.

Hildegard of Bingen. Directed by Lisa Belcher-Hamilton. Pioneers of the Spirit series. New York: Trinity Television, 2005.

The Unruly Mystic: Saint Hildegard of Bingen. Directed by Michael M. Conti. North Boulder, CO: Michael Conti Productions, 2015.

Vision: From the Life of Hildegard von Bingen. With Barbara Sukowa. Directed by Margarethe von Trotta. New York: Zeitgeist Films, 2011.

Websites

Abbey of the Arts (http://abbeyofthearts.com). This website provides a variety of online, self-study retreats, including retreats on Hildegard of Bingen. In-person retreats to Hildegard's Germany are also available.

Benedictine Abbey of St. Hildegard (www.abtei-st-hildegard.de). The current Benedictine abbey with ties to Hildegard's legacy, located in Rüdesheim, Germany.

Healing Chants (www.healingchants.com). Meditation, music, and other resources related to Hildegard.

Hildegard Publishing Company (www.hildegard.com). Publishes sheet music of the works of women composers, including Hildegard.

The Hildegard von Bingen Project (www.sequentia.org/projects/hildegard.html). Information on Sequentia's work related to Hildegard's music.

International Society of Hildegard von Bingen Studies (www.hildegard-society .org). A broadly based organization and clearinghouse for those interested in Hildegard.

Internet History Sourcebooks Project, Fordham University: The Life and Works of Hildegard von Bingen (http://legacy.fordham.edu/halsall/med/hildegarde. asp). Reliable history database for all periods; includes a section on Hildegard.

Land der Hildegard (www.landderhildegard.de). A historical site (in English) with information on Hildegard, information for visitors, and more.

Leonarda Productions (www.leonarda.com). Publishes the work of women composers, including Hildegard, in modern notation.

Pierre-F. Roberge's Discography (www.medieval.org/emfaq/composers/hildegard.html). Lists many recordings of Hildegard's music.

St. Hildegard of Bingen (www.hildegard.org). Information and articles on Hildegard.